TM

Prints and Impressions

by Paul Mauro and Robin Epstein
with H. Keith Melton
consultant

Scholastic Inc.
New York • Toronto • London • Auckland • Sydn
Mexico City • New Delhi • Hong Kong • Buenos Aires

ISBN: 0-439-57177-4

Design: Mark Neston

Illustrations: Daniel Aycock, Yancey Labat, Antione Clarke

Photos: Mark Neston, Lightning Powder Company (pages 18, 21, and 38)

12 11 10 9 8 7 6 5 4 3 2 1 3 4 5 6 7 8/0

Printed in the U.S.A.

First Scholastic printing, December 2003

The publisher has made every effort to ensure that the activities in this book are safe when done as instructed. Children are encouraged to do their detective activities with willing friends and family members and to respect others' right to privacy. Adults should provide guidance and supervision whenever the activity requires.

Case Log

When you see this symbol throughout the book, you'll know to use your **detective equipment** in the activity.

When you see this symbol throughout the book, you'll know there's a related activity to be found on the Detective Academy **website**.

The Power of Prints!

Gotcha, rookie detective! Just by opening this book, you've provided the police with enough evidence to prove you're trying to learn their tricks. Unless you were very sneaky, as soon as you touched this book's cover, you left your **fingerprints** all over it! You see, when a **perpetrator** commits a crime, he almost *always* leaves behind some evidence—and fingerprints are about the best evidence a detective can find at a crime scene. In many cases, the perp might as well have left behind his name and address!

Why are fingerprints so powerful? Because everyone's got 'em and everyone's are unique. And since fingerprints don't change over the course of your life, even if someone starts a life of crime in the second grade, guess what? If her prints are properly lifted and stored, that perp could be identified from the prints she left as an eight-year-old when she's an eighty-year-old!

Visible print. Latent print.

Fingerprints fall into two categories: visible or latent. **Visible prints** occur if a perpetrator has muddy, bloody, or otherwise dirty hands, and he leaves an obvious print that's easily seen. **Latent prints** aren't detectable to the naked eye, and they need to be "recovered," or made visible, by using special techniques to lift them off a surface. (You'll learn about these shortly.)

But finding fingerprints is only *half* the battle—detectives have to match them, too. When a detective recovers a fingerprint, he needs to match it to prints that are already on file—otherwise, all he has is another mystery to solve (as in: *Who did this fingerprint come from?*). In the U.S., the Federal Bureau of Investigation (FBI) stores records of fingerprints in its massive computer database. So when a new print is found, a detective, using a computer, can compare it to fingerprint records on file. If he finds two that are the same—he has a match. And now, a name to go with those prints!

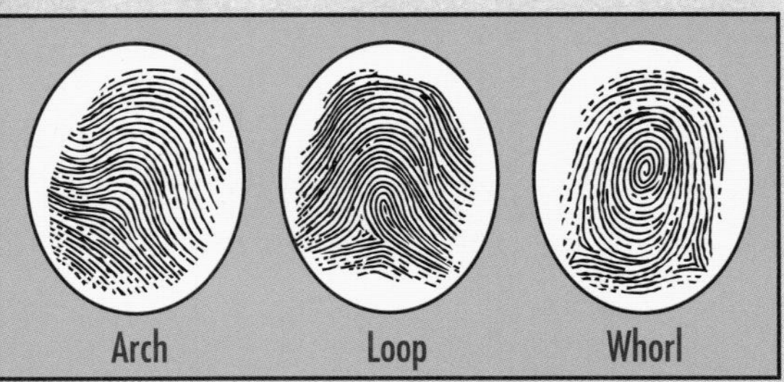

Matching prints isn't as simple as it sounds (even with computers). There's a whole scientific classification for the different traits in fingerprints and, in this book, you'll learn those fingerprint categories, including **arches**, **loops**, and **whorls**. Before you know it, you'll be "reading" prints like a pro!

The second half of this book will focus on *another* type of evidence a perp could leave at a crime scene: **impressions**. Impressions can be any number of identifying marks that the perp leaves behind, ranging from tire tracks to footprints to bullet holes to **tool marks**.

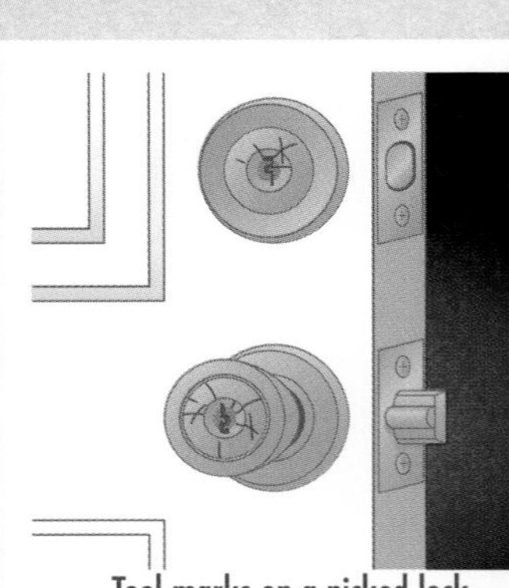

Tool marks on a picked lock.

(For instance, if a perp used a screwdriver to force entry into someone's house, he'd leave tool marks on the door.) Impressions can come in all different varieties—and, like fingerprints, can provide a detective with excellent clues. If she knows how to read them!

Finding good prints and impressions—and then analyzing them—is no easy task. But once you develop your detective's eye for spotting them, you'll find pritns and impressions everywhere. You'll almost feel like you're living in one big crime scene!

Tire marks made by a getaway car.

Detective Equipment

In order to help you lift and record prints of suspects and criminals, here's this month's special gear:

Inkpad, to blacken a person's fingerprints before recording them.

Print Cards, where you'll record a person's prints for analysis.

Black Powder, so you can dust over an area that you suspect may contain invisible prints.

Magnetic Print Wand, which will help you apply the proper amount of black powder to the area where you're looking for prints.

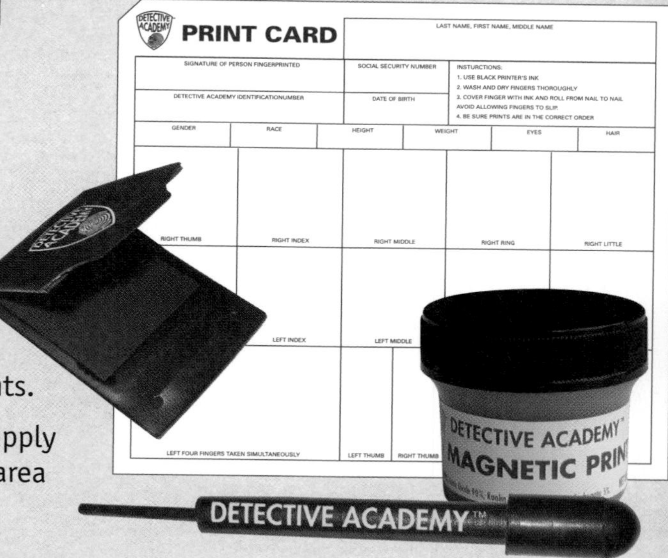

By the way, rookie, if you practice printing so much that your inkpad runs out of ink, just ask a senior detective to help you secure another one. Though it might look slightly different from the one you get in this kit, inkpads can be found at most stationery stores. (And to preserve the ink, remember to keep your inkpad's cover closed until you're ready to use it again.)

Detective Academy Website

Hey, rookie—want to learn more about fingerprints and impressions? Just hop online at **www.scholastic.com/detective**. This month's password is: **loopsnwhorls**. Each month, a new password is assigned to give you special clearance to the Detective Academy website, and to make sure no one unauthorized gets in!

PASSWORD: LOOPSNWHORLS

Working the Scene: Prints and Impressions

Hey, rookie—there's been a theft at the museum in town!

In the middle of the night, it seems a **perp** pried open a long-unused window in the rear of the famous Avery Art Museum, then loaded up a truck with priceless masterpieces and took off! Check out the scene below as detectives and crime scene technicians check for **prints** and **impressions**!

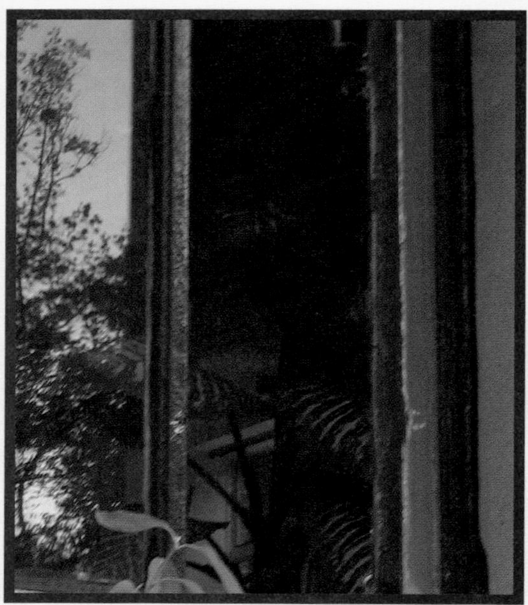

Tool Marks

These tell-tale marks occur when a perp uses a tool to force his way in. By prying open a window (as shown) or a door, the perp will *always* leave an impression of the tool he used.

Visible Prints

chnicians look for fingerprints made in dust or any her bloody, dirty, or greasy substance that will hold clear impression of the perp's prints.

Footprints

No matter how careful a perp is, his feet have to touch the ground! Footprint impressions can be an excellent clue—so detectives make sure to photograph them for later examination. In fact, a plaster cast can be made of footprints, which will allow detectives to obtain a permanent, three-dimensional version of them.

Latent Prints

e scene techs know that just because fingerprints aren't le, that doesn't mean they aren't there. Any place the is likely to have touched—like, for instance, the bar he used to open the window—will be dusted for ible latent prints.

Tire Tracks

Impressions made from a vehicle's tires can provide detectives with another valuable clue. Like footprints, these impressions are photographed, and can be preserved by making a permanent plaster cast of them.

Like every other part of detective work, prints and impressions have their own special language! As you go through the book, whenever you see a word or phrase in boldface, check here to find out what it means.

Arch: A fingerprint pattern that consists of a single raised "bump."

Elimination Print: A fingerprint taken of someone who was at the scene of the crime—and who left a set of his prints there—but who is not a suspect in the case (like the victim).

Fingerprints: A term used to describe the pattern of skin ridges at the tips of your fingers (often shortened to "prints").

Forgery: A crime in which a perp falsifies written information in order to steal.

Friction Ridges: The distinguishing lines on the skin that are the basic building blocks of its fingerprint pattern.

Impressions: Identifying marks that a perpetrator leaves at a crime scene, such as footprints or tire tracks, generally in a soft surface.

Latent Prints: Prints that are invisible to the naked eye and have to be lifted from a surface through the use of special powder or another technique.

Live-Scan: A computer-generated fingerprint image.

Live Scan Imaging System: A machine used to electronically scan fingerprints.

Loop: A fingerprint pattern in which the ridges form a series of half-circles, one inside another.

Loupe: A very small magnifying glass.

Partial: Part of a print that may still be useful for purposes of identification.

Perpetrator: A person who commits a crime (often shortened to "perp").

Plain Arch: A pattern in a fingerprint that has a side-to-side flow of ridges with an "unremarkable" arch near the middle.

Print Cards or Ink Cards: A paper or cardboard file on which you can press and save fingerprints.

Raised Prints: When prints are invisible and you dust them, they become visible—or raised.

Ridges: The raised portion of the skin that defines a print.

Rolled Impression: When a finger is rolled across an ink card or the Live-Scan imaging system to record a fuller impression of the print.

Tented Arch: A pattern of fingerprint in which the ridges look like they're flowing upward at a 45-degree angle or greater.

Tool Marks: The indentations or scratches left in a surface by a device—like a hammer or screwdriver—when it was used to force something open.

Visible Prints: Fingerprints that are obvious to the naked eye because they've been coated in a substance like grease or blood.

Whorl: A fingerprint pattern in which the ridges form a series of circles, one inside another.

Keep Your Ear to the Ground

Stuff You'll Need

- Willing family members or a few friends
- String
- Ruler
- Notebook DA
- Pencil DA
- Tape

Hey, rookie—did you know that using **fingerprints** to catch criminals didn't start in America?

In 1901, the most advanced detectives in the world worked in England's famous Scotland Yard. It was these forward-thinking detectives who first pioneered the use of a fingerprint system to identify and pursue **perps**. While some American law enforcement groups began to experiment with using prints soon after, it wasn't until the 1920s that the FBI set up their state-of-the-art national fingerprint file. Today, the world's most extensive and advanced print lab is located at the FBI identification center in West Virginia, where millions of fingerprint records are currently stored.

Before fingerprints were used, though, investigators worked with a system to identify criminals, which was created by a French man named Alphonse Bertillon. The Bertillon System relied on the comparison of particular body parts that have distinct features—like, for instance, the ears and eyes. If you really look at them, you'll see that people's ears and eyes actually are unique to each individual. Some people have big ears, some very small, some have droopy lobes, others virtually no lobe at all. (And this is to say *nothing* of the different things people have *in* their ears—but let's not go there!)

Want to see just how unique everyone's ears and eyes are?

What You Do

Part I. Listen Up!

1. To warm up your powers of observation using the Bertillon System, take some notes on the distinctive qualities of your family members' ears. Does your mother have an extended lobe? Do your father's ears stick out? Has your sister had her ears pierced—and if so, how many times? Be as specific as possible in your descriptions. Once you've noted these characteristics, start taking some actual measurements of

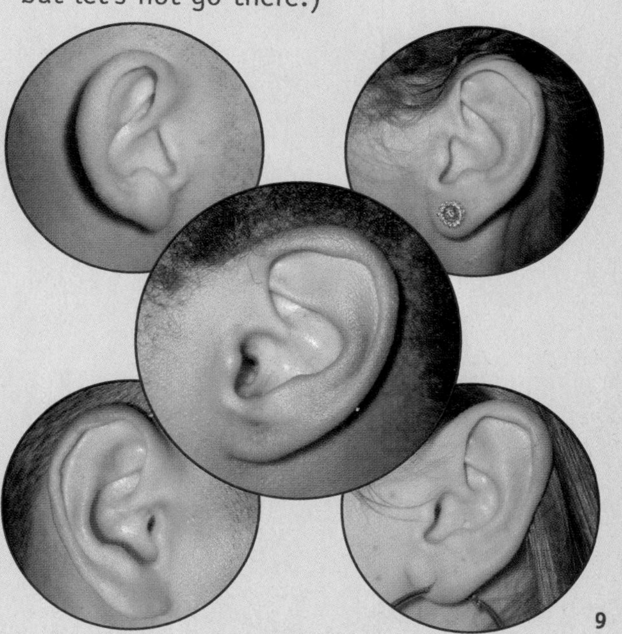

their ears with a piece of string. (Since the ear is neither flat nor straight, it's easiest to get its dimensions first by using string, then measuring that string against a ruler later.) Measure the ear from top to bottom and from side to side, as well as the length of the lobe, and the size of the little "button" that sits in the middle of the ear.

2. If you want to see how well you did, wait a day or two. Then ask one of your subjects to let you examine their ears again. Compare their ears to your original notes. Did you catch everything the first time? Are there any parts that you missed? If you had to identify this person using *only* the description you wrote of their ears, could you do it? And here's another question for you, rookie: Why do you think fingerprints are a better identifier for the police to use than ear prints? Check *Case Closed* at the book's end for your answer!

Part II. Eye Spy

Though Bertillon primarily relied on measurements of the ears, he also looked at other distinctive traits, like the color of the eyes and the distance between them. Let's see how specifically *you* can describe these traits!

1. Sit one of your rookie friends or a family member down and look him in the eye. What color eyes does he have? Brown eyes are the most common, but as you've probably noticed, not all brown eyes look the same. That's because every eye color can have a different shade to it. (Sometimes a person can even have eyes of two entirely *different* colors!) You can see that some brown eyes are flecked with green, some are striped with a yellowish color, and some appear so dark that they look almost black. How would you describe your rookie friend's eye color? (If he has blue eyes, are they sky blue? Bluish-green? Dusted with a darker blue tint?)

2. Now take a look at yourself in the mirror. (You're one good-looking rookie, aren't you?) Write down as accurate a description as you can about the color of your eyes, as well as the shape of the entire eye area. Are your eyes perfectly round? Slightly oval? Almond shaped? When you've been as specific as possible, ask your friend to describe to you your eye color and shape as specifically as he can. Did he use any of the same words and descriptions that you did?

3. Now take out your string and measure the distance between your rookie friend's

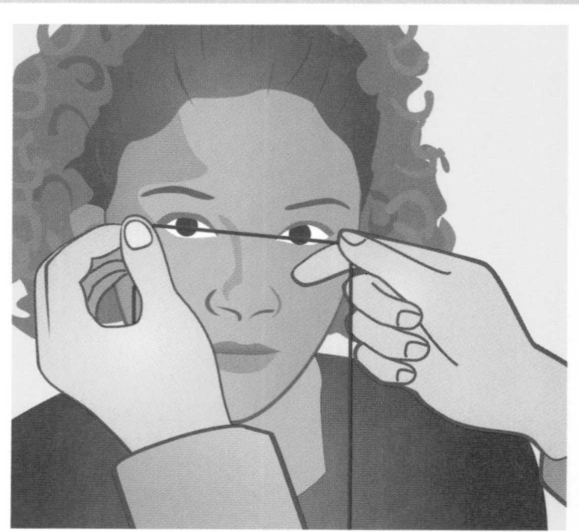

eyes, then have him measure between yours. Whose eyes are farther apart? Do another set of measurements from the arch below the eyebrow to the top of your hairline. Who has a bigger forehead?

Part III. Measuring Up

1. Use your string to get some other measurements, too. What's the distance between your wrist and your elbow? Between your elbow and your shoulder? Which part of your arm is longer? Is the same true for your rookie friend?
2. Get a long piece of string and tape one end of it to the tip of your middle finger on one of your hands. Now stretch out both of your arms from end to end. Have your friend stretch the string attached to the middle finger of the one hand across your chest to reach to the tip of your middle finger on the other hand.

(Just like an eagle, this measurement is known as your "wing span.") Go ahead and measure the length of that string now. Does the number look familiar to you? It should—because your wing span is the same as your height!

What's the Real Deal?

Did you see, rookie, that while comparing ear measurements, it's possible to identify someone by using just a *part* of their body? Because every person is unique, it's possible to tell eveyone apart by examining just a particular body characteristic—like ears, for example, or fingerprints. This activity should have shown you how important it is for a good detective to stay alert to these differences in people's appearance. Even if the Bertillon System is no longer in use, the concepts are still important—especially when attempting to identify someone from a description, or when writing up a description of a perp for a crime report.

In real life, ear prints are not usually considered useful evidence by law enforcement because there is no central "ear print" file to compare them to! But Bertillon's identification system was important because it introduced the practice of taking body measurements from arrested perps in order to keep track of them. From there, it was a short jump to setting up the fingerprint system in use today. In many ways, it's Bertillon who is responsible for today's identification system—he just chose the wrong body parts!

Case File #2

Stuff You'll Need

- Magnetic wand
- Black powder
- Tape
- Index cards
- Pen

The Big Dust Up

Rookie, no matter how clean your home is, if you look closely enough, you'll realize that there are **fingerprints** everywhere. Depending on the type of surface (and how recently it was cleaned), some prints are going to be easy to see, while others will become observable only after they've been treated with powders or special chemicals. For a detective working a case, this is both good and bad news. Why?

Since prints remain largely invisible to the naked eye, most **perps** fail to realize they've left evidence of their presence all over the crime scene—that's the *good* news. So even if they wipe their fingerprints off the "obvious" places, like a doorknob or a window, perps often forget about other areas they touched. But the *bad* news with print invisibility is exactly that—they're invisible, so they're hard to find! Because investigators won't immediately be able to see all the prints left behind, the whole crime scene must be gone over with a fine-tooth comb (or, in this case, a magnetic wand!) to make sure no critical evidence is missed.

In your *Basic Training Manual,* you identified surfaces and objects that were likely places to find fingerprints (such as a window, a mirror, the television set, and so on—remember?). You used your magnifying glass to examine those spots and you located the fairly obvious prints. Now, however, it's time to step it up a bit. It's time to "magnetize" your print skills further by using your black powder and magnetic wand to shade otherwise unclear fingerprints with color, making them visible to the naked eye.

What You Do

Part I. Your Fingerprints Are All Over It!

1. Find an "easy" surface in your home, like a glass table, a counter, or a tabletop, and press your fingertips on it. (Since you'll be using black powder, it would be best to work on a light or clear surface to make the contrast better.)
2. Take your magnetic wand and dip it into the black powder. Keep the wand's silver plunger pressed down toward the rubber part to activate the magnet—the powder will cling to the rubber tip.
3. Now, by pulling up on the silver plunger, dump the powder from the wand over the area where you left your prints. Swirl the powder around the area using the wand, and then pick up the excess powder by activating the magnet

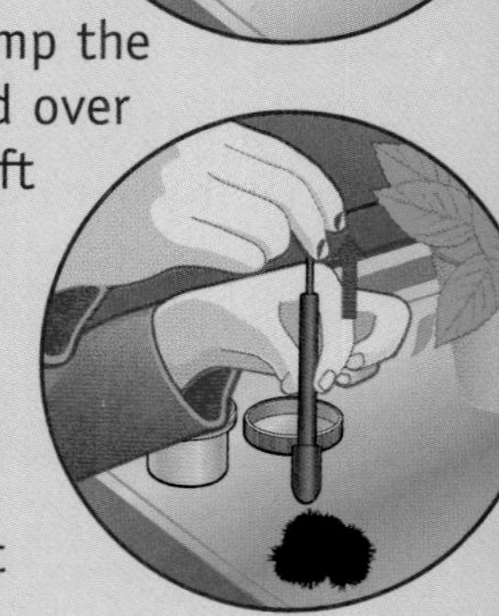

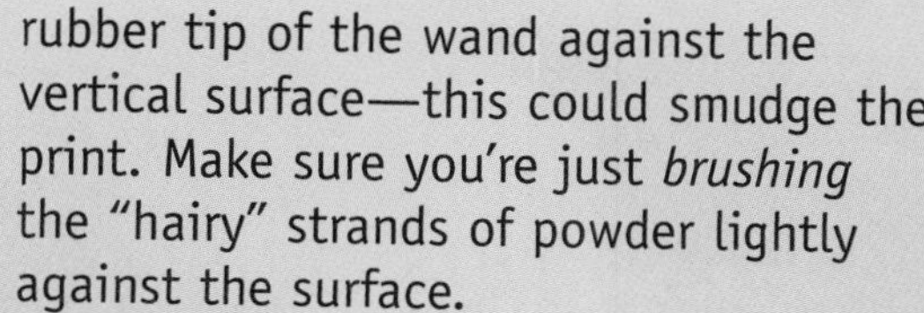

again. When you've collected as much of the surplus powder as you can, dump it back in the jar for future use.

4. Take a look at the area you've just "dusted." Your fingerprints should be clearly visible!

Part II. Climbing the Walls

Because perps leave prints in all sorts of places at a crime scene, you need to be able to pick up this evidence even when it's on a vertical surface—like a window or a door. Try this:

1. Press your entire hand and palm against a window.
2. Load up the magnetic wand with the black powder again, but this time, instead of dumping it on the surface (since it's vertical, all the powder would just fall to the floor!), gently brush the wand against the window, as if you're painting a canvas. While you're holding the wand in one hand, hold the powder jar in the other so you can keep it underneath the area you're dusting. This way, you can catch any loose powder that might fall and make a mess (we want to avoid making any senior detectives angry!). Be careful: While you're dusting this area, you also want to make sure you avoid rubbing the rubber tip of the wand against the vertical surface—this could smudge the print. Make sure you're just *brushing* the "hairy" strands of powder lightly against the surface.
3. You should now be able to see your palm print. If you can't, try it again—but this time, run your hand through your hair or around your face before you press it against the window. Then follow the same steps as before. Did it work better this time? Think you know why? (You'll see why in a bit!)
4. Now try other types of prints, like the edge of your palm—or even your lips! As strange as it may seem, perps leave a variety of prints at crime scenes, and investigators want to gather as much evidence unique to the perp as possible. So because various parts of your skin contain those crucial **friction ridges**, even prints left by chapped lips can serve as identification!

Part III. A Sticky Situation

Okay, detective—you've **raised** some **prints**, making them visible to the naked eye. Now what? Well, those prints could be a key piece of evidence—so you aren't just going to leave them at the crime scene! In order to have a record of the prints you raise, you'll need to lift them off the surface and store them, so they can be analyzed later.

Want to see how it's done?

1. Take a piece of tape and—sticky side down—place it over the fingerprint you raised in *Part I* or *Part II*. Rub your finger gently across the top of the tape to "capture" the print, then carefully pull up the tape. Can you see the print now transferred to the tape?
2. On an index card, note the date, time, and exact location that you found the print—then attach the tape with the lifted print onto the card. Now, just like real detectives, you've started a fingerprint file!

What's the Real Deal?

Contrast is the key to developing images of **latent prints**, which is why black powder is used so frequently against light-colored backgrounds, like white walls, glass surfaces or cream-colored appliances. But a variety of colored powders also exists so that the police can get the best possible contrast on backgrounds of differing colors. Some of these powders even contain "fluorescing" elements, which make them glow ("fluoresce") under special light. But regardless of the type of powder you use, it's always important to examine prints under strong light because it helps the eye see the contrasts better.

Temperature can also play a part in how well the magnetic powder adheres to a latent fingerprint. Under warmer temperatures, the oils in the residue of many fingerprints can become softer. Powder tends to stick better to these softer residues. So, it may be more difficult to get away with a crime in a hot, sunny location as opposed to a cold, snowy one!

Rookie, you should have learned in this activity that the process of fingerprinting depends on a number of factors. One of the things that will affect how clear a dusted print will be is the amount of skin oil present in the print. The more sweat and oil deposited on a surface the person has touched, the more the powder will cling to the fingerprint, and the more visible the print will become.

But as you've already learned, fingerprints are only good evidence if they can be matched to someone. When the police take a print off a surface, that print is converted from the removal tape to a photographic image that is stored in a computer. The computer then runs a check to see if the print can be matched to someone whose prints are already on file.

DET. HIGH-TECH!

The Eyes Have It!

You know, rookie, your fingerprints aren't the *only* completely unique part of your body. The truth is, *all* of you is unique. But some body parts are better to use for fast identification purposes than others. For crime scene techs, fingerprints are obviously the best, because perps often leave them at a crime scene. But if you just want to *identify* someone—that is, figure out exactly who they are—then believe it or not, fingerprints are *not* the best way to go. Your eyes are!

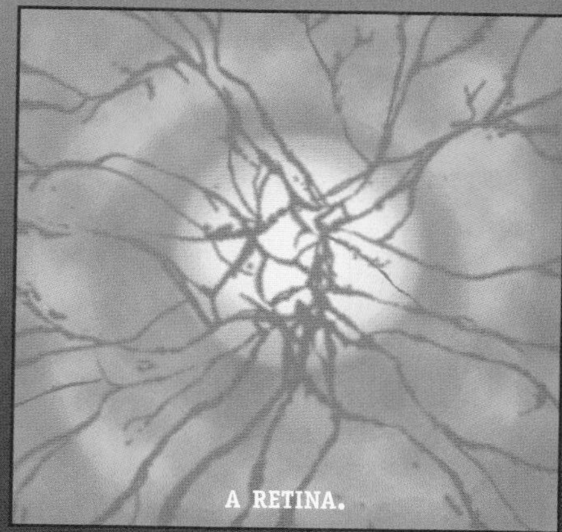

A RETINA.

As you may have learned in science class, your eye consists of a few different parts (the *iris*, the *pupil*—you've heard these terms, right?). Another part of your eye is called the *retina*. You can't really see your retina—it's behind your pupil (the dot in the middle of your eye) and your iris (the circle around your pupil—the part that gives your eyes their color). But even though you can't see it back there, a computer can! And that's how retinal identification works.

In 1935, two scientists doing eye research discovered that every person has a pattern of capillaries—that is, tiny blood vessels—that run through their retina. And this pattern is totally unique in everyone—no one has the same pattern. Even identical twins.

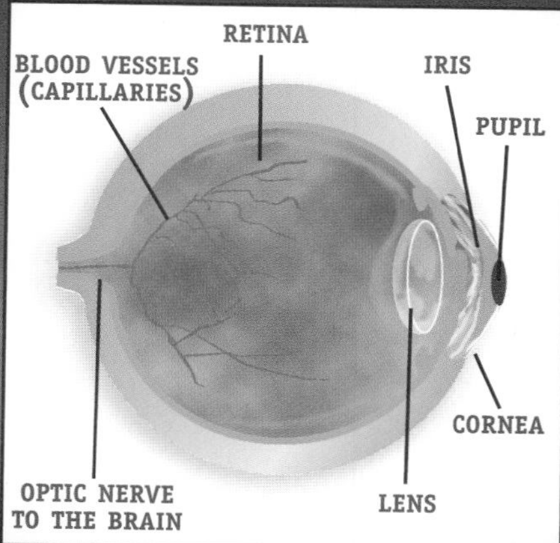

Eventually, this discovery was put to use. With a retinal scanning machine, a person only needs to look into a camera-like lens, and a computer takes a quick picture of the capillary pattern in that person's retina. The computer then compares that pattern with the pattern they have on file for that person. If it's a match—the person is identified!

Retinal scanners aren't in widespread use in law enforcement—but they are widely used in the security field. In places like banks, spy agencies, and high-tech businesses—places that will only let people they know and trust inside—retinal scanners are becoming more popular.

And even though it's doubtful that retinal scanners will be used any time soon by most detectives, the records gathered by retinal scanning machines can be very valuable to an investigation. Once a person has had their retina scanned, it places them at an exact place at an exact time. And because retinal prints are pretty much impossible to fake, that's about the best alibi there is!

Case File #3

Stuff You'll Need

- Paper towel or cloth
- 2 drinking glasses (use glass instead of plastic, if possible)
- Soap
- Hand towel
- Magnifying glass DA
- Flour
- Plate
- Vegetable oil, bike grease, or potato chips
- Washcloth
- Rookie friend

One Greasy Slimeball

You know, rookie, it would make it much easier for detectives if criminals *inked* their fingers before they went to a crime scene. But as you know, this never happens (unless you're dealing with the world's dumbest **perp**!). Still, as you've learned, a perpetrator's fingers are *always* coated in the natural oils present in his skin—whether or not he realizes it.

And since the more oil you have on your fingertips, the more likely you are to leave a complete **print**, you can think of these natural body oils as a way of "greasing the wheels" of print identification.

Try this to see how it works:

What You Do

Part I. Grease Monkey

1. Wipe two glasses clean with a paper towel or cloth, so that they're clearly print-free.
2. Pick up one of the glasses and handle it as you would if you were about to take a drink from it. Then, put it down on the counter in a safe place so you can examine it later.
3. Now go wash your hands thoroughly with soap and dry them off (make sure they're really dry!). Right after you've finished drying your hands, pick up the second clean glass and handle it the same way as you did the first. When you're finished, set the second glass next to the first one.
4. Take a look at both glasses using your magnifying glass. You touched both in exactly the same way—with exactly the same hands—but does one of them have more clear prints on it than the other? Why do you think that is?

Part II. Let Your Fingers Do the Walking

Sometimes, rookie, perps leave so many clues at a crime scene that it can seem as if they're *trying* to get caught! So give this a try, and see how a perp who's a slob can make a detective's life easy!

1. Put a little flour on a plate and stir your fingers around in it. You want to make sure your fingers are coated with flour, but you should tap off any excess so you don't wind up leaving a flour trail around your house!

2. Now walk over to the nearest refrigerator or medicine cabinet and open and close it a couple of times, making sure you're using both hands. Then take a look at the marks you've left.

3. You should be able to see a set of visible prints without having to use your magnifying glass. But now take that magnifying glass out anyway and look a little closer at your "flour-y" prints. How clear are they? Can you spot the **friction ridges**?

4. Start experimenting with some other substances like vegetable oil, grease from your bike chain, or hair gel. You can even use a bag of greasy potato chips (if your mom says no, tell her you're eating them to further your investigation!). Spread these substances (one at a time) around your fingertips. Then find a surface that'll be easy to wipe clean when you're done (like a glass table, mirror, or even the inside of the kitchen sink), and try leaving some visible prints. Which substances leave the clearest prints? Which leave the fuzziest set of **visible prints**?

5. Now grab a washcloth and clean off all the prints you've just left. Remember, ultimately a good detective always wants to keep all evidence of his own presence out of a crime scene!

Part III. Reading Palms

1. Is it possible for a perp to pick something up *without* leaving her fingerprints (and without cheating by using gloves)? Challenge a fellow rookie detective to do this as the two of you lean over your bed. Place a drinking glass on the bed and tell her to try to pick it up without using her fingers.

2. She'll probably realize that the best way to pick it up is by holding her fingers out straight and grasping the glass between her palms. But does she think she can get away without leaving any evidence? Well, not so fast!

3. Take a look at that glass again. Though there may not be a fingerprint, your friend probably left *another* type of

identifying marker—a print of her palm! In fact, you can **raise** her palm **print** using the same techniques you use to raise normal fingerprints.

JUST THE FACTS

Palm Reader!

LAST NAME, FIRST NAME, MIDDLE NAME | DATE OF BIRTH | SOCIAL SECURITY NUMBER

GENDER | RACE | HEIGHT | WEIGHT | EYES | HAIR

(RIGHT)

PALM PRINT CARD

Palm prints can be captured on print cards like the one shown here—they're just like the fingerprint cards you have, only for palm prints.

Hey, rookie—hold out your hand and look at your palm. See all those lines and wrinkles? You don't have to be a fortune-teller to "read" them—you just have to be a trained detective!

Believe it or not, the pattern on your palm is as unique and distinctive as the one on your fingerprints. In fact, your *own* two palms don't exactly match up. (Don't believe it? Take a very close look!) Because palm prints are so unique, they make excellent evidence. If a detective can obtain a palm print from a crime scene—and then match it to a suspect—that evidence is considered as good as fingerprint evidence. And rookie, that's about as good as it gets. Case closed!

The problem with palm prints, however (and why they aren't more widely used), is that there's no central file for detectives to consult—and with fingerprint technology so advanced, there isn't likely to be a "national palm print database" anytime soon. So if a detective has a crime scene palm print—but no suspect to match it to—that evidence won't be very valuable.

But if that detective *can* develop enough information on a suspect to match the suspect's palms to the print, the case is solved. *Hands* down!

What's the Real Deal?

Not leaving a fingerprint is tougher than you might have imagined, huh rookie? You should have seen in this activity that the sweat and natural oils that your body produces will strongly affect how clear a print you leave. Even if you don't usually *see* these oils (you don't usually *feel* them, either), they're there—and there is often just enough of them left behind for fingerprint powder to cling to. In normal, every-day life, you usually leave these little oil deposits on everything you touch. Washing your hands might remove your skin oils for awhile—but it's not very long before they're back. And a good thing, too. Otherwise, all a perp would have to do before committing a crime would be to wash up, and he'd never leave any prints!

Remember, not *all* fingerprints are made this way. In real life, a perp could leave a print in something sticky, or even in dust, and it would be *more* visible than the fingerprints you just experimented with. But usually, real crime scene techs spend most of their time searching for **latent prints**, like the ones you just left on those drinking glasses. Latent prints are the most common form of prints—and the toughest to find. It's one of the reasons that processing a crime scene is a special skill in itself, requiring special crime scene techs. Unless they're trained in it, even most *police officers* can't find and raise latent prints!

Case File #4

Analyze This!

Stuff You'll Need
- Magnifying glass

Now that you know how to collect and store **fingerprints**, rookie, you need to be able to analyze them, too. (After all, if you don't know how to do that, what's the point of collecting them?) Ready to learn how?

Fingerprints are classified into three basic groups based on the patterns they show. They are:

1. **Arch:** The arch is the simplest pattern, and there are two basic types: the **plain arch** and the **tented arch**. The plain arch has a regular "side-to-side" flow of **ridges**, with a low arch near its center. The tented arch has a steep slope of ridges in its middle, almost resembling a "soft" triangle.
2. **Loop:** The second print group is the loop. It looks just like what you'd expect: a looping curve that goes up, turns completely around, and comes back in the same direction. If the loop comes from the right side, it's called a *right-side loop*. If it comes from the left side, it's called a *left-side loop*.
3. **Whorl:** The third major category of fingerprint types is the whorl. There are four basic types of whorls: the *plain whorl*, the *central pocket whorl*, the *double loop whorl*, and the *accidental whorl*. Each of these patterns has specific identifying markers, but basically, a whorl makes some kind of circular pattern in its center. If a fingerprint doesn't fall into any of the first three whorl categories, it's designated as an accidental whorl (which sounds more like a dangerous amusement park ride, doesn't it?).

Obviously, rookie, there are a whole bunch of possibilities with fingerprints. The best way to get a feel for how to separate the different types is to practice with them a bit. So let's get started!

Plain Arch

Tented Arch

Left-Side Loop

Right-Side Loop

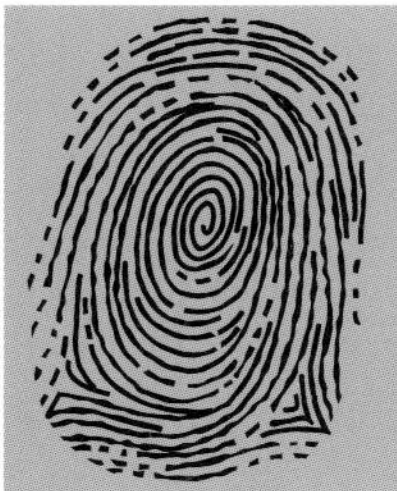

Plain Whorl

Central Pocket Whorl

Double Loop Whorl

Accidental Whorl

What You Do

Part I. Concentration, It's Not Just a Game...

Though detective agencies will usually use a computer to match prints, it always comes down to the judgment of a real live human being whether or not a print is truly a match (after all, computers *do* make mistakes, you know). The best investigative tool is always your detective brain. So let's give it a whirl (not to be confused with a *whorl*).

1. This is a fingerprint recently collected at a crime scene. Can you match it to one of the prints stored in the FBI's national fingerprint file below? Remember to examine the print for loops, whorls, arches, and other distinguishing characteristics. Check out *Case Closed* to see if you've made a match.

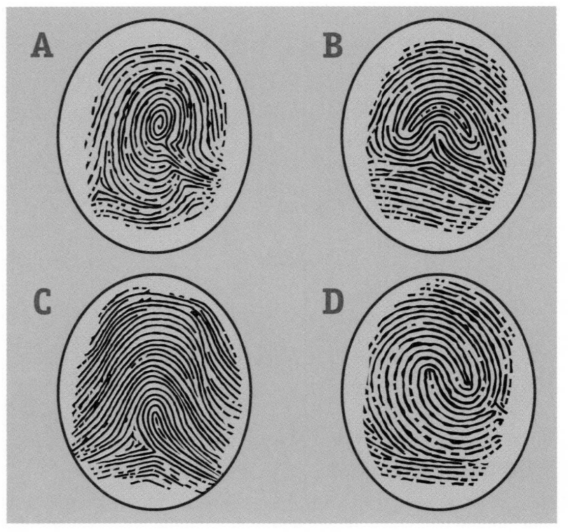

Part II. Concentrate Harder!

1. Thought the first one was easy? Try this. These prints are much closer to one another, and in order to differentiate between them, you'll need to examine them more carefully. Frequently, a detective will use a magnifying **loupe** for a task like this, so you might want to use your magnifying glass to make the ridge patterns bigger.

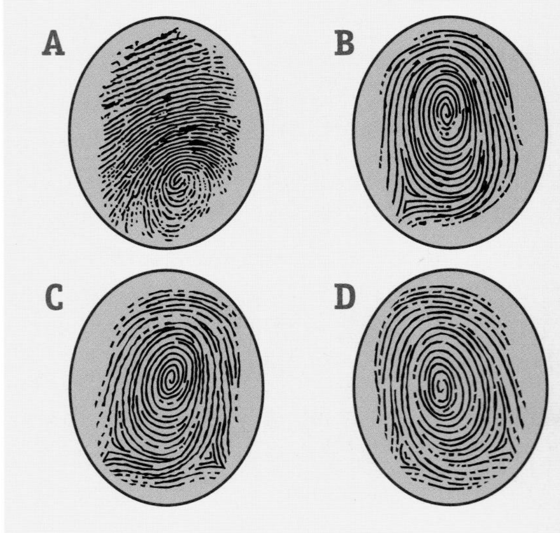

2. Once you've identified a match, can you tell which of the three main fingerprint categories this **perp's** print falls into? Check *Case Closed* to see if you're right.

More From Detective Squad

For more practice with the eight fingerprint types, log on to

www.scholastic.com/detective.

What's the Real Deal?

Did you see, rookie, how matching fingerprints to samples that are on file often comes down to recognizing the patterns within those fingerprints? That's the reason the study of prints can get so technical. In order to match them accurately, print techs must be able to recognize those loops, whorls, and arches. Some fingerprints from different people can be pretty close in appearance—so a print tech has really got to be on her toes. You should have seen in this activity how print matching can come down to the tiniest detail—and how it takes a trained and experienced eye.

Real police officers use computers to speed up the matching process, but it still can be slow, difficult work. Also, computers often don't return an *exact* match of a print—they'll return a few of the *closest* matches to your original crime scene print. It's then up to the expertise of a print technician to go that extra step and make that one definite match that gives detectives a name to go with the print—and a perp to collar (or arrest) for the crime!

Just the Facts

Watch Those Prints!

Once fingerprint evidence has been recovered from a crime scene, it's important to handle it properly so that it can be used to its greatest effect while prosecuting the perp with the crime. Fingerprints go through a "chain of custody" after they're lifted from a scene to make sure the integrity of the evidence is maintained. The chain usually follows this order:

- Evidence is recovered and documented at the crime scene.
- A field patrol officer or a fingerprint specialist transports the evidence to the crime lab for processing.
- The crime lab then assumes "custody" of the evidence.

The best way to get print evidence to the crime lab is to package it in paper and then to seal it up. The paper allows moisture surrounding the print to evaporate, preventing the print residue from degrading, and sealing it prevents other **latent prints** from being introduced.

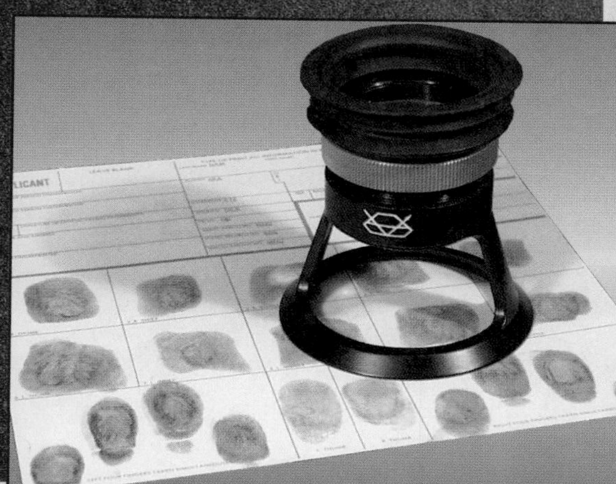

Detectives use magnifying loupes like this one to study prints on a print card—looking for a match.

Case File #5

Filing It Down

Stuff You'll Need

- A few rookie friends or family members
- Print cards DA
- Pen
- Inkpad DA
- Soap
- Cloth
- Black powder DA
- Magnetic wand DA
- Tape
- Index cards

So far, rookie, you've done some excellent work lifting the **perp's** prints from the crime scene, and in beginning to analyze them, too. But by this point, you know that unless you can match those prints to a set that already exists in a police database, those **fingerprints** reveal about as much as the wrapped birthday present you found at the top of your parents' closet. You know you've got something there—you just don't know what it is yet!

Fortunately, as you learned earlier, the FBI holds the largest database of prints in the world. (Too bad they don't also keep records of your parents' birthday purchases!) If the criminal you're looking for has a police record, his information is already stored in that FBI computer, and it can be called up at any point for identification purposes. So as soon as someone's been arrested and booked, they're forever after tracked in the system. And, if you've ever been printed for something government-related, even if it had *nothing* to do with a crime—say, to apply for a job at the post office or to join the military—chances are those prints are on file as well.

It's a safe bet that if you start keeping a file of prints, like those of your friends and family, they'll think twice before poking around in your bedroom while you're out and about!

What You Do

Part I. Ink Marks the Spot

1. First, convince one of your family members, or a fellow rookie, to play the "suspect" for this activity. Once you've lined up your first suspect, start gathering information about him on your **print card**. You'll need to write down the person's first name, middle name, and last name. You should also record the person's gender (male or female), race, height, weight, eye color, and hair color.

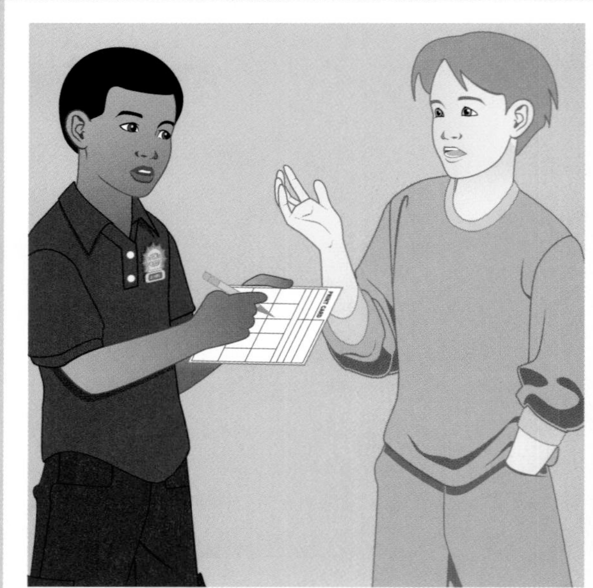

2. Now begin taking the prints of your suspect's right hand. Lift the cover of your inkpad and press the person's

fingertips onto the ink, making sure the tips get completely blackened. Do one finger at a time. You need to roll the entire fingertip, from one side of the nail to the other, as shown in the picture. As you can see on the card, the different boxes indicate which fingerprint is supposed to go where, so roll the person's corresponding finger into each box.

3. When you've finished recording the prints of the right hand, do the same thing for the left.

4. Now, at the bottom of the card, take the prints of all four of the suspect's fingers at the same time. Do one hand at a time by pressing the suspect's four fingers onto the inkpad, then onto the box at the card's bottom. Remember: Those prints will look slightly different than the single fingerprints because they won't be **"rolled impressions."**

5. To make your file as complete as possible, ask as many friends and family members to participate as you can. If you run out of print cards, you can always go online to the Detective Academy website at **www.scholastic.com/detective**, where you'll be able to print more!

6. As soon as you've finished printing your suspects (and before they touch anything), make sure they wash the ink off their hands with soap and water!

7. Hey, rookie, be sure to fill out and file a print card for yourself, too!

Part II. To Catch a Thief!

Now that you have everyone's prints on file, it's time to use them to solve a "crime." First, you need to prepare the crime scene: the bathroom—more specifically, the medicine cabinet. Since medicine cabinets are usually mirrored surfaces, they record prints especially well. Start by wiping the mirror with a cloth, making sure you've removed any existing prints.

1. Tell three of the suspects whose prints you've previously recorded to go into the bathroom one at a time. Before they do, have them discuss among themselves who will touch the medicine cabinet to leave his prints on it—but tell them not to tell you who'll be doing the "break in."
2. When they're done, dust the mirror for prints just like you did in *Case File #2: The Big Dust Up, Part II* (dusting on vertical surfaces—remember?).
3. Did you find anything? If so, now you'll want to lift those prints off the mirror as you learned how to do in *Case File #2, Part III*. Once you've lifted the print with tape and secured it to an index card (making sure you've labeled it properly), it's time for the analysis.
4. Just like detectives do, you'll need to compare the print you've lifted against the file of prints you began putting together in *Part I* of this activity. (Hopefully, you rolled the prints of your friends in *Part I*.) Do you see a set of matching prints? If so, can you state with confidence that you've identified your perp? Good work, rookie!

More From Detective Squad

One of the benefits of keeping a record of your family's fingerprints (including your own) is that if your home is ever broken into, you'll be able to offer the police a handy set of **elimination prints**. This will immediately show crime scene techs that the prints they just found on the refrigerator belong to your mom, say—and not to a hungry thief!

What's the Real Deal?

Rookie, you should have seen in this activity how important it is not only to be able to lift prints, but also to match them to a well-maintained, up-to-date fingerprint file. Even if you're an expert at lifting prints and analyzing them, if there's nothing to match them with, you're out of luck!

Today, the police have literally millions of fingerprints at their disposal, with more added all the time. Every police agency in America can access the FBI's computerized print file, and do so without leaving the station-house! By using high-speed transmission wires, police can transmit the fingerprints to be checked to their own state-wide fingerprint database, as well as to the FBI national database.

It's hard to imagine that not too long ago, print matching was all done by hand. It's just another example of how technology has helped law enforcement stay one step ahead of the perps! (To find out exactly how all this technology works, check out *Detective Hi-Tech!—Live Scan*, coming up next.)

DET. HIGH-TECH! Live Scan

Hey, rookie—ever had a pen leak ink all over you? Have you ever handled the toner cartridge from a printer? Did your hands end up covered in ink? Didn't care for the experience, did you? Well, neither do detectives!

In the old days, detectives taking fingerprints had to use an inking process that was sometimes slow and messy. First, the perp's fingers had to be run through ink, then placed one at a time on an ink card (just like you did in *Case File #5: Filing It Down*). The print cards were then stored in a file cabinet. Think about how many people get arrested each day, and you have some idea of how huge a central national fingerprint file would be!

A Live Scan machine.

If, in the past, detectives recovered unidentified fingerprints from a crime scene, they had to go through thousands of previous fingerprint cards, looking for a match.

But beginning in the late 1970s, a different technology began to emerge to change all that. By using a computer that *scans*—that is, takes a fast picture of—a person's fingerprints, detectives could fingerprint a perp without ink. The prints would be scanned by and stored in the computer—making a **live-scan**. No mess, and no piles of files!

But computerized fingerprint machines—generally called **Live Scan Imaging Systems**—really became valuable when they were hooked up to the FBI's "AFIS"—the Automated Fingerprint Identification System. In the late 1990s, the FBI developed software that allowed police departments all over the country to hook into AFIS, giving them access to millions of print records from all over the nation.

Prints are scanned by placing your fingers here.

As a result, detectives everywhere in the U.S. can now not only run a perp they're fingerprinting through the AFIS in order to identify him, they can also run prints found at a crime scene to see if they can get a match.

It was the biggest advance in fingerprint technology since fingerprinting started. And *really* bad news for perps!

Case File #6

Your Very Own Collection Agency

Stuff You'll Need

- Hole punch
- 3 white index cards
- Pen
- String
- Rookie friends and family members
- Black powder DA
- Magnetic wand DA
- Tape
- Magnifying glass 

You learned in *Case File #4: Analyze This!* about the classification system that exists for the three main patterns in **fingerprints**. And now that you've collected a file of your own prints, as well as those of your friends and family, it's time to analyze where they fit into this system. Does your best friend have a **tented arch**? Is your sister a central pocket **whorl** girl? (If she is, you might not want to say it to her face!)

Sometimes it's hard to remember what you have among the various categories (**arch**—plain or tented), **loop** (right slope or left slope), whorl (plain, central pocket, double loop, or accidental). Refer back to the pictures on page 19 to help with your IDs.

What You Do

So, rookie, where are you going to keep the classifications of all the different fingerprint types you've analyzed?

Part I. Book It, Rookie!

1. Start making a print reference flip-book by punching holes in the corner of three white index cards.
2. At the top of each card, label it with the name of each fingerprint type, that is, arch, loop, or whorl. Remember, for arch, you'll have to draw a line dividing the card in two, and label one side plain arch and the other tented arch. Same for loop; whorl will need four spaces on the card.

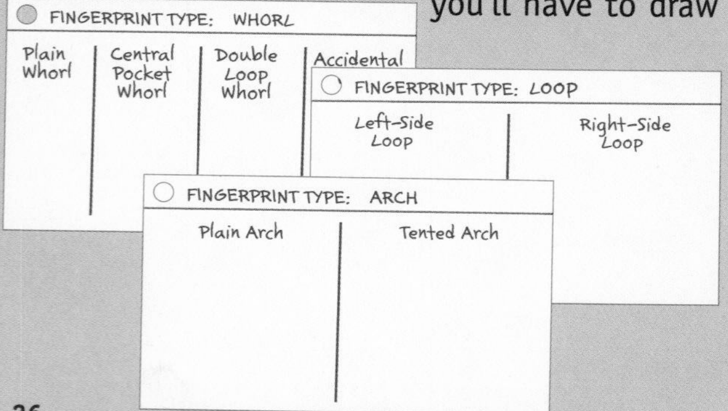

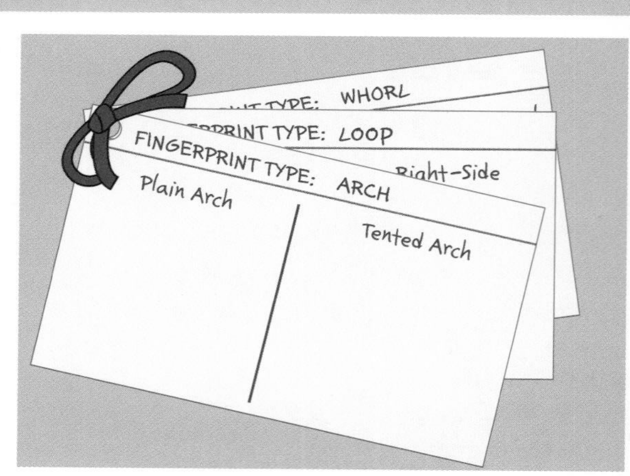

3. Place a string through the holes at the top of the cards and tie it off. Okay, rookie, now that you have your book, it's time to fill it in! (Don't do anything yet. See *Part II*!)

Part II. Eye Spy

1. Start analyzing the patterns among the prints you took on your print cards of family and friends from *Case File #5: Filing It Down*, using your magnifying glass.
2. Compare the prints against the pictures on page 19, which have the three different fingerprint patterns.
3. When you've found matches for each fingerprint category, get that friend or family member to leave prints for you to dust and then lift. Place that fingerprint onto the corresponding card in your print reference flip-book. You now have a handy reference for each type of fingerprint category!
4. Don't get discouraged if you can't find matches to all the fingerprint types right away. It's very possible that you won't be able to find them all among your family members or fellow rookie detectives, so you might need to venture out and print others in order to fill all the categories. But remember, rookie, detective work requires hard work and dedication, so keep it up. The prints are out there, so go find them! (And don't forget to analyze your *own* fingerprints!)

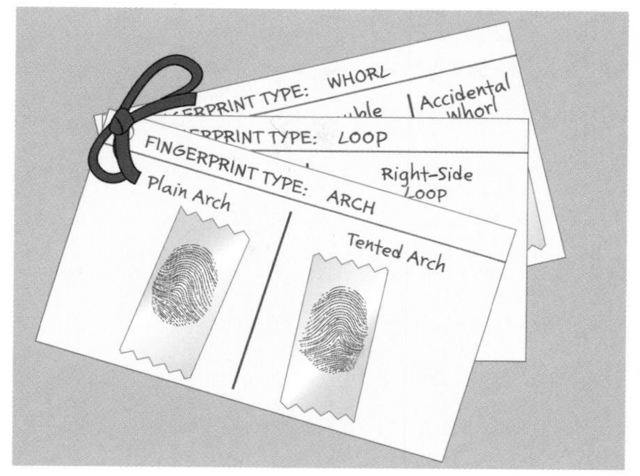

What's the Real Deal?

In this activity, rookie, you should have seen how the different types of print patterns aren't just something to read about in a book—they're real, and they exist right around your house! By practicing identifying and lifting prints in these different categories, you're developing your "crime scene eye," and before you know it, you'll be able to tell the different print types apart—without having to look at the references. It's the first step toward making a positive identification!

In real life, print types vary a great deal and, as you saw, each of the main print categories you've practiced with has sub-categories—making for even more variety! That can make it tough to match prints exactly. It's one of the reasons why crime scene technicians are such a highly trained part of law enforcement. They have to be!

Case File #7

Forge Ahead!

Stuff You'll Need

- Senior detective
- Black powder DA
- Magnetic wand DA

If there's one thing you can always predict, rookie, it's that detective work is unpredictable! You never know what could end up being an important clue. Depending on the crime, just about anything you think of could have print evidence on it!

For instance: What if you were investigating a **forgery** case? Forgery is a crime in which a perp produces a false document—for example, he makes a fake driver's license—so he can claim to be someone else. Just by writing false information, he's committing a serious crime!

Another way perps commonly commit forgery is by signing someone else's name to a credit card receipt or to a check. Here's how the check process works: When a store accepts a check from a customer, it's as good as cash. That's because the storeowner then takes that check to a bank, and the bank gives the storeowner cash for it. The bank will then take the money for the check out of the customer's bank account. The person who wrote the check still pays for whatever they bought—it's just delayed a bit. And using a check is safer than walking around with pockets full of cash all the time!

But what if the customer who pays for something with a check is not who they say they are? What if that person signs "Bill Thomas" to the check, but he's really someone else? When the store takes the check with Bill Thomas's name on it to the bank, one of two things can happen. The first is that the name is made-up and the check is fake and the bank won't have any idea who "Bill Thomas" is—so nobody gets paid! Or second, there actually *is* a real Bill Thomas, and someone *else* has been pretending to be him (perhaps they've stolen his checks or made up checks using his name). In that case, the real Bill Thomas ends up paying for something that a forger has just bought!

So what do you think is a great way to investigate who it is that's out there forging signatures on checks? That's right—dust the checks for **prints**!

What You Do

Part I. Check It Out!

1. First, ask a senior detective (in this case, a parent would be best!) to let you use one of their blank, unused checks. (Make sure the check has VOID written across it—this means that it can't be used at a store if it's accidentally lost.)

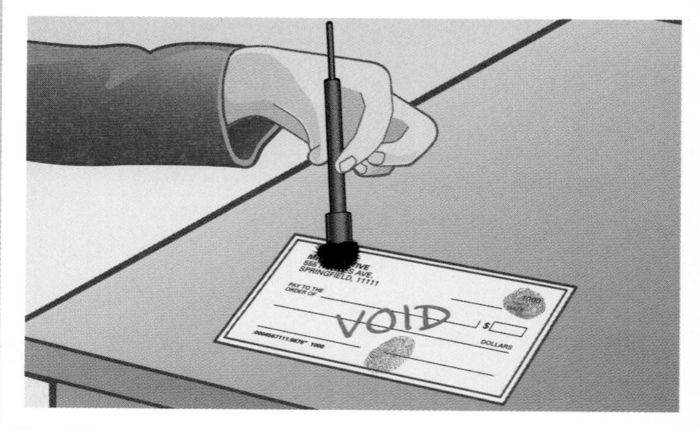

2. Using your black powder and magnetic wand, dust the check for prints. At first, don't dust the whole thing—try to anticipate where a person using a check might have left prints. For instance: Checks come bound together in little booklets. So to tear a check out, most people grab it by the edge—usually near a lower corner, on the front of the check. (Ask your senior detective to show you how this is done.)
3. After you've tried the edges, dust the whole check. Did you come up with any prints? Don't forget to dust the back of the check, too. After all, anyone who handles a check also touches the back of it!

Part II. Cancel That Crime!

1. Now ask your senior detective for a cancelled check—that is, a check that has already been legally used, and so can't be used again.
2. Dust this check the same way as you did in *Part I*. Did you find some more prints? How many different prints can you identify?

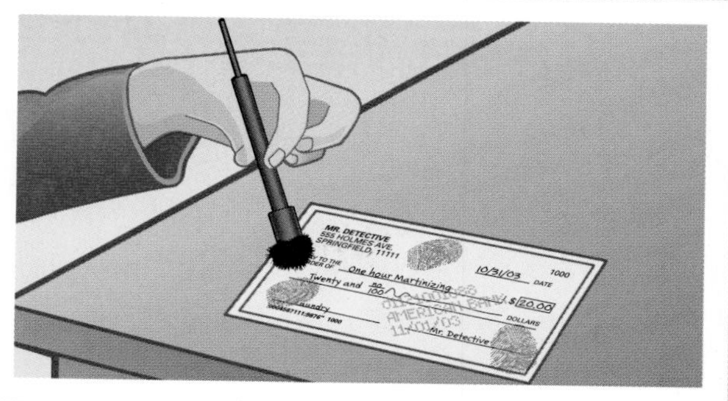

Part III. All in the Family

1. Remember, in *Case File #5: Filing It Down*, when you put together a fingerprint file of your family? Pull out that file!
2. Using the cancelled check from *Part II*, can you find any prints that match to a family member? Who do you think the other (unidentified) prints are from? Check *Case Closed* for a hint.

What's the Real Deal?

Did you see in this activity, rookie, how fingerprints can be used to establish a "chain of custody"? Chain of custody is really just a fancy legal term for the list of people who had possession of something (in this case, a check). If you had been investigating a real forgery, you could have gained valuable clues by identifying whose prints were on that check—and so, who had been in possession of it at one time.

If you found this activity difficult—don't worry. Even real CSI techs don't love dusting for fingerprints on paper—it isn't easy! But in a case of check forgery, if nobody remembers what the perp looked like or if he wasn't caught on a surveillance camera—a fingerprint might be the best clue you have. And just by going one step further and eliminating the prints from non-suspects (the check's owner, the bank employees), you could eventually wind up with just the perp's prints! (Pop quiz, rookie, do you remember the term **elimination prints**?)

Case File #8

Stuff You'll Need

- A fellow rookie
- Magnetic wand DA
- Black powder DA

Go to Your Room!

You know, rookie, technicians don't have time to waste. In most police departments, there aren't really enough techs to go around (a good future career choice, by the way—you'll always be employed!). Because they're so busy, crime scene techs often don't waste valuable time printing an *entire* crime scene. They don't really have to. Experienced techs *know* where they have to dust for **prints**—they know which spots a **perp** is likely to have touched while at the scene.

What a perp touches can usually be determined by the nature of the crime. For instance, for something like an auto theft, techs know to check things like the car door and the steering wheel. As you learned in *Case File #7: Forge Ahead!* for a **forgery**, a good spot to start is on the document itself—in *Case File #7* it was the check that the perp forged someone's name on.

Let's see if you can use logic and find some likely spots to dust for after a home burglary!

What You Do

1. You've been assigned to investigate a home burglary that occurred last night. Your first step: Visit your fellow rookster's house, and ask to see his room (that's right—invite yourself over!). This bedroom is going to be the crime scene!
2. Now, before you start dusting, ask yourself: Where would a perp who has burglarized this room leave prints? Consider: How did the perp get in? What was he looking for? What would he touch as he tried to find whatever he was looking for?
3. Now, dust the areas you think a perp is most likely to touch during a burglary. (Remember something else, too: If a perp got in—he's also got to get out! What did he touch on his way out?)
4. Make sure that when you're done, you clean up after yourself. Remember: To you it's a crime scene, but to your friend, it's his room!
5. Next time, switch roles, and have your friend over to your house. Who found more prints? A little competition never hurt anyone! (When you're both done, check *Case Closed* for some likely spots for success when dusting at a home burglary.)

More From Detective Squad

With the permission of a senior detective, try dusting another room in your house. Where do you find prints there? Any surprises?

Try dusting in some unusual places—for instance, in the family room, pull a book out of a bookshelf, and dust the front of it. Has someone read it recently? Can you compare the fingerprints to your "family print file" and determine who last read this book? Next time you see them, surprise the reader by asking how he enjoyed the story!

CASE IN POINT

The Power of the Print!

Rookie, it's amazing how much detectives can learn from a single fingerprint. Those little loops and whorls pack a lot of power!

In January of 2000, CSI techs in Seattle, Washington, were called to a crime scene by detectives in order to try to recover evidence from a stolen vehicle, which had been found. It was a tough job—the car wasn't revealing much in the way of evidence. Then the techs checked the rear-view mirror. At some point during the getaway, the driver must have reached up to adjust it for a better view behind him—unwittingly leaving a **partial** fingerprint that expert techs were able to recover.

On the strength of that single partial, detectives collared two perps for the stolen car. When they discovered several other stolen cars during the investigation, they realized they had stumbled onto a major car theft ring!

Then it got even better. When one of the perps was being printed for his arrest, detectives discovered his prints matched those of a perp wanted for two bank robberies in a nearby city!

All those cases were solved—and all from just a single partial print. Do you see why fingerprint evidence is taken so seriously? Prints can be about the best clues a detective can get!

What's the Real Deal?

Did you see in this activity, rookie, how *where* you dust can be an important decision? If you think about it, dusting an entire crime scene would be an awfully time-consuming job—even a small room has so many surfaces and edges, it would take a whole team of techs quite a while to handle it all. And when they'd be done, they'd have so many prints, it would take *another* whole team just to process all the prints for matches! So you should have seen that a big part of the skill of fingerprinting is using your head as well as your hands.

In real life, this is exactly how printing works. True, at a very serious crime scene, techs will be more thorough—they will not only print what they figure the perp touched, they'll dust other areas, too. They might even dust areas outside the immediate crime scene—let's say, in a phone booth down the block, if they think the perp might have made a call there before committing the crime. In some cases, techs will really go all out!

But in most cases, that's not routine—not because techs are lazy, but because it's not necessary. The majority of times, if there are prints at the crime scene, the techs will know pretty quickly where they are—they've done this before, they're experts. They not only know *how* to look, they know *where* to look. And whether you realize it or not, little by little, you're becoming an expert, too!

Case File #9

Stuff You'll Need

- A rookie friend
- A pair of sneakers or shoes with a thick rubber sole
- Magnifying glass DA

See You Later, Gaitor

Have you ever seen someone walking down the street and you just knew who it was before you even saw his face? That's probably because you were remembering that person's *gait*—that is, the way he walked. Up 'til now, rookie, you've learned all about **fingerprints** in this book, but now it's time to zoom in on **impressions**!

If you pay close attention, sometimes you'll find that a person's gait can be as distinctive as the color of his eyes. Some people take very small steps when they move, while others cover a lot of ground with each step. Some people swing their hips, some shuffle their feet, and some are even "pigeon-toed" (so their feet turn in toward one another). All these factors have an impact on the type of footprint impressions a person leaves behind.

So maybe you can identify your friend walking toward you at a hundred paces. Good going! But here's another challenge: Can you identify how he's walking from the tracks he leaves behind?

What You Do

Part I. The Weight of the Gait

1. Invite a rookie friend over and tell him to wear his sneakers. (Rookie, you go get your sneaks on, too!)
2. Go to a playground area or someplace you're likely to find a large space of packed dirt, like a baseball diamond. Tell your friend to start leaving different types of footprints by doing the following: walking, hopping, sprinting, and walking backward. Make sure you've got your back turned, rookie, so you can't tell when he's switching his gait!
3. When he's finished, start comparing the various prints. How do they look different? Can you tell when your friend was walking backward? Any idea why there's a difference in the spacing of the prints when he walked backward as opposed to forward? (Hint: Try it out yourself before you answer and then check out *Case Closed*!)

4. Now switch roles, and *you* leave various types of footprints while your friend turns away. You can experiment with different kinds of walks, too: a flying leap, pretending you're jumping over puddles, a side-to-side shuffle, or see what would

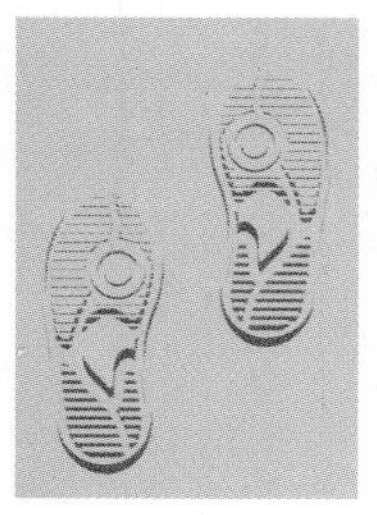

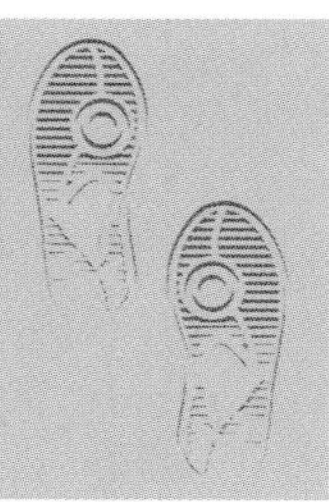

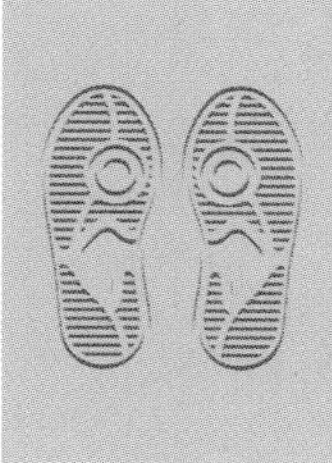

happen if you tried walking with a limp. Let the other rookie know when you're finished making your prints. (And be sure to tell him the kinds of walks you did before he tries to guess which one's which!)

Part II. On the Surface

1. If you're near a beach, try this activity in the sand. Can you see clean prints? Are there any problems you can imagine in trying to measure someone's gait in the sand? (Hint: What do you think happens if there's a windstorm? Check out *Case Closed*.)

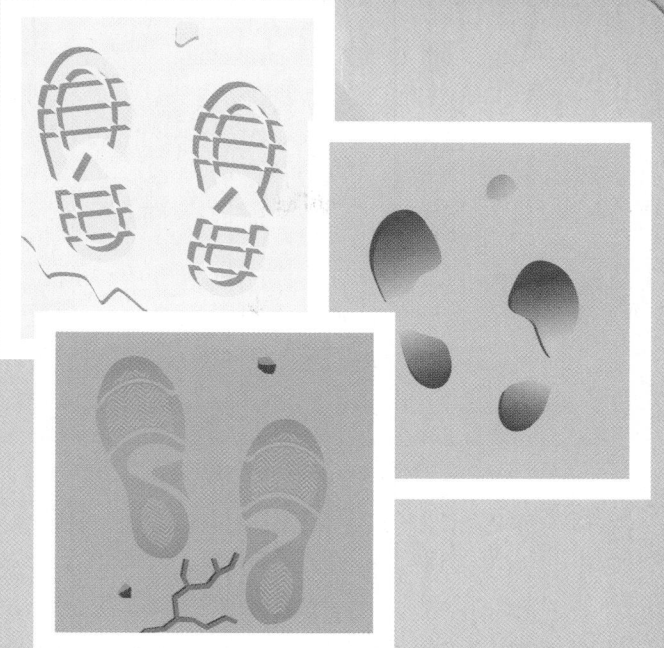

More From Detective Squad

Next time it snows, see how your footprints track on snowy surfaces.

What's the Real Deal?

In this activity, rookie, you should have seen that footprint evidence can be a good clue in a number of ways. For instance, the way a person walks (his "gait") can have a great effect on the footprint evidence he leaves. If the **perp** walked around the crime scene, the deepest impressions his foot would leave would be around his toe and heel. However, if he were running, the toe area would leave a more signifcant mark because a person doesn't usually pound down on his heel while he's sprinting. Also, when a person is running, his footprints will be spaced farther apart than normal, and they will show more weight because you take larger steps while running, and you press the ground harder.

Or say your perp had injured his leg or walked with a limp. The footprint would probably show a "drag," and would clue detectives in on one of the perp's most distinguishing characteristics.

In this activity, rookie, you should also have seen how footprints can vary not only by the *way* the person walked but by the *different surfaces* the person walked on.

By carefully examining different footprints—even those made by the same person—a detective can tell a lot about what that person was doing. And that's information real detectives love to have!

Case File #10

Stuff You'll Need

- Your sharp rookie min

Let Your Footprints Do the Talking!

Well, rookie—think you're ready for some more footprint analysis? Below are a few examples of footprints made on various surfaces by different people. Remembering wh you learned in *Case File #9: See You Later, Gaitor*, can you decipher these **impressions**

What You Do

1. What can you tell about *how* this person was moving, rookie?

2. What made these strange tracks?

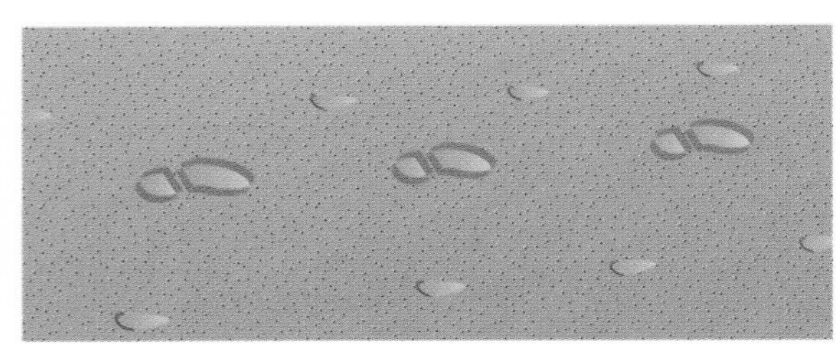

3. Who do you suppose made these impressions along the beach?

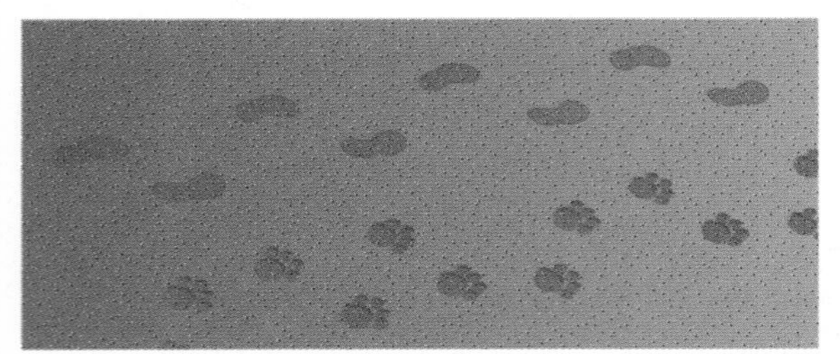

4. How about these footprints made in shallow dirt?

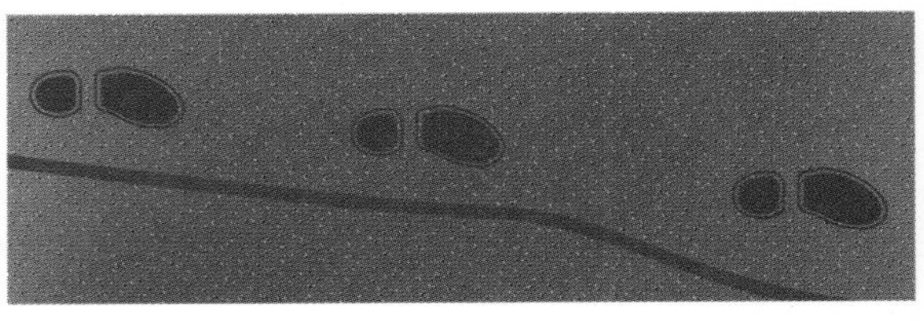

5. And see if you can figure out something about the person who made these tracks!

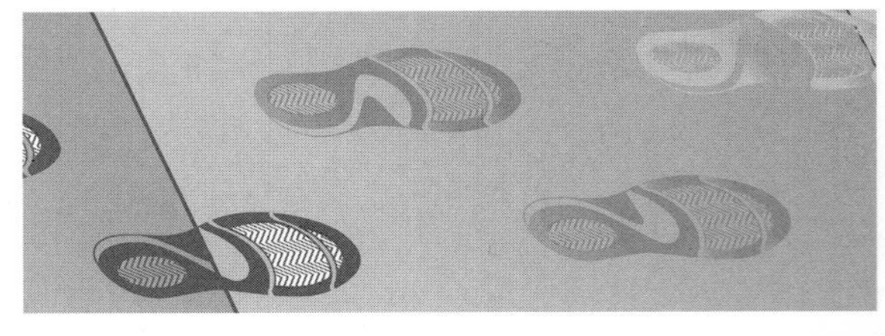

Answer Box:

A. A teenager riding a scooter

B. A child walking a dog

C. A person walking first, then running

D. A basketball player who just walked through a puddle

E. A person on crutches

Check *Case Closed* to see if you figured out how each set of footprints were made, and also to see how a detective would analyze these prints.

Case File #11

Shoes from Paris... Plaster of Paris!

Stuff You'll Need

- Boots or shoes with deep treads or thick soles
- Scissors
- Cardboard—4 sturdy pieces (try using an empty shoebox if possible)
- Petroleum jelly
- Senior detective
- 1 cup of baking soda
- 1/2 cup of cornstarch
- 2/3 cup of warm water
- Saucepan
- Mixing spoon
- Paintbrush

High tops. Pumps. Tennis shoes. Loafers. Flip-flops. Sandals. Boots....

In police work, the shoes people wear are evidence that could tie them to a crime scene! If footwear evidence is properly processed, it can often be used to reveal the type, make, model, and size of the shoe that someone was wearing while committing a crime. Additionally, the footprint **impressions** left at a crime scene can help investigators determine the number of suspects involved, the way they entered and exited the area, and the manner in which they moved around the scene.

But by examining footprint evidence, not only can detectives learn how a **perp** *moved* at a crime scene, they can also learn a lot about the perp himself. Remember—just like you and most of your friends, perps can be pretty particular about what they wear on their feet. And that can lead to vital clues for a sharp detective!

Because the police can learn so much about a perp from his footwear, crime scene techs have special techniques for preserving footprint evidence. Aside from photographing footprints, techs can also pour plaster into the impression a perp's foot made in soft ground—and come away with a perfect replica of the **print**. This can then be taken from the scene for further examination and investigation.

Want to see how it's done?

What You Do

Rookie, this activity is made up of three parts. The first part requires setting up the mold around your footprint. In *Part II*, you'll be making a plaster of Paris mixture. And in *Part III*, you'll pour the plaster mixture into the mold to fill in your impression. For *Parts II* and *III*, you should work under the direction of a senior detective because you don't want to accidentally wind up with a cast *on* your foot instead of a cast *of* your foot!

Creating your footprint impression will work best if the area in which you choose to lay your track is soft or moist. But you don't necessarily need to wait for a rainy day to do this activity; if it hasn't rained for a while, or if you live in a place where it just doesn't rain very often, you can make your own mud by watering a patch of dirt. If you do this, though, don't drench the spot by adding too much water! The mold won't hold if the area is too wet. Just try to get the ground soft enough so that you can mold it, like clay.

Ready to begin?

Part I. Make a Good Impression!

1. Locate a nice soft spot of ground outside where you'll be able to leave a solid foot impression. Wearing rubber boots or thick-soled shoes (ones with distinct patterns are best), step hard and make a footprint in that spot.

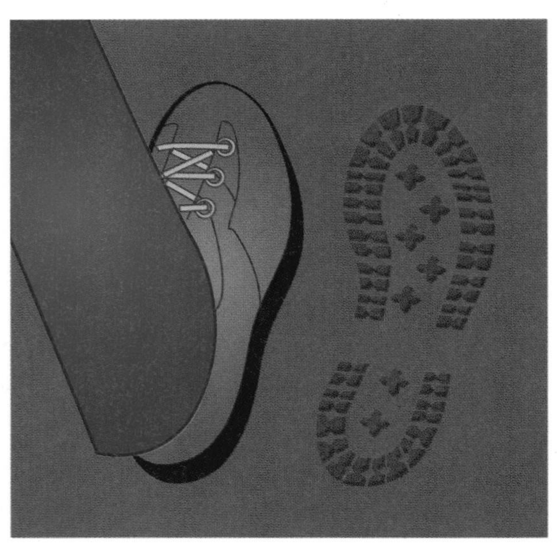

2. Now cut your cardboard into four pieces—two of them should be just longer than the length of your shoe print, and the other two slightly wider than the width of the impression.

3. Now apply petroleum jelly to one side of each cardboard strip. The reason you're doing this is because once it's time to remove the plaster of Paris cast from the mold, the slickness of the petroleum jelly will help the cast slide out more easily. (If you've ever baked a cake, it's the same concept as greasing a cake pan before you spoon in the batter and put it in the oven.)

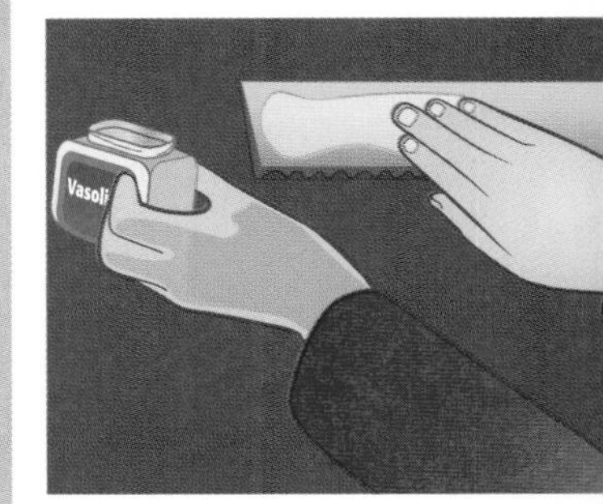

4. Set the four pieces of cardboard around your footprint (making sure the petroleum jelly side faces in) and push them down into the ground. You want to make sure the corners of each piece of cardboard are touching so that when you've finished setting it up, it looks like a rectangular-shaped baking pan surrounding your footprint. Now head toward the kitchen to start preparing the plaster of Paris mixture you'll be pouring into this mold.

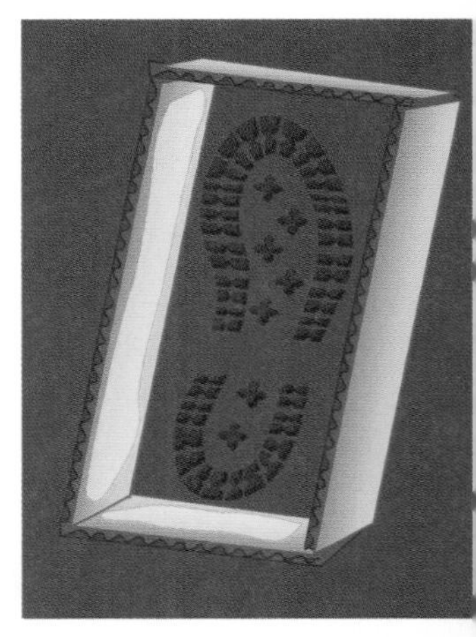

Part II. Mixing It Up

1. With your senior detective, follow the recipe to make the plaster mixture.

   INGREDIENTS:
   1 cup of baking soda
   1/2 cup of cornstarch
   2/3 cup of warm water

2. Mix the baking soda and the cornstarch together in a saucepan.
3. Add the water and stir the mixture over medium heat until it becomes smooth.
4. Now turn the heat up to boil the mixture, and keep stirring! Stir for about two to three minutes. The mixture should thicken a little, but still remain liquid.
5. Let the mixture cool a bit, then move on to *Part III*!

Part III. Fill These Shoes

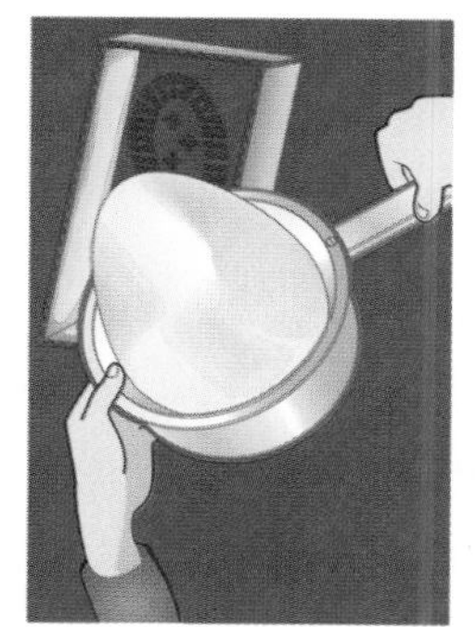

1. Take your plaster mixture outside and pour it into the mold you set up in *Part I*.
2. Let the plaster dry in the mold for about an hour. You want to give it enough time to dry before you try lifting it out of the mold—otherwise you could wind up with a "broken foot" print.

3. Using the sides of the cardboard mold to grip the plaster, lift the cast out of the ground and remove the cardboard around it. With your paintbrush, gently brush off any loose soil or dirt that stuck to the footprint cast.

4. Look at the bottom of your mold and compare it to the bottom of your shoe. How good is the match? Would you be able to identify your shoe based on the impression you just made?

More From Detective Squad

Invite some fellow rookies over and ask them to leave footprint evidence outside (remember to tell them to do this in soft ground). Before they come inside, tell them to take their shoes off and leave them in a pile by the door. Now have them tell you where they've left their footprints. Take molds of the impressions they left. Can you match the impressions to the bottom of each shoe? Are there any giveaways that you can see in the cast of the soles, like a Nike "swoosh" logo or a distinctive waffle pattern?

What's the Real Deal?

Did you see, rookie, how pouring the warm plaster mixture into the footprint allowed you to end up with a perfect copy of that print? As with most things in life, timing is everything. You should have seen that if the footprint you made was nice and visible, and you got the mixture ready in time—it was a simple matter of pouring and waiting to get yourself a valuable piece of evidence!

Detectives know that before the police arrive at a crime scene, the perpetrator is often the last person to leave the scene. So when first responders secure a crime scene to be processed by detectives and techs, special attention needs to be paid to footprint evidence, so that it remains uncontaminated. After all—you don't want to make a perfect cast of a footprint, only to discover it belongs to one of your fellow detectives!

Just the Facts

First Steps

Making casts of footwear impressions started in 1786 in Scotland, and police all over the world still rely on some of those original techniques today. Plaster of Paris continues to be widely used for making casts, but in 1986, the FBI started recommending the usage of "dental stone" for casting purposes. Dental stone was ultimately determined to be better than plaster because, in addition to being more durable and harder, it was easier to clean, and so less likely to lose detail from the cast's surface.

This footprint cast—made using dental stone—is stored in an evidence box.

Don't Tread on Me!

Stuff You'll Need

- 3 rookie friends
- 3 different bikes (ask each rookie to bring his own)
- Spray bottle
- Pencil DA
- 3 sheets of white paper
- Magnifying glass DA
- Scissors
- Cardboard
- Petroleum jelly
- Senior detective
- 1 cup of baking soda
- 1/2 cup of cornstarch
- 2/3 cup of warm water
- Saucepan
- Mixing spoon
- Paintbrush

As you've seen, rookie, footprints can provide great information to the police about a suspect—and, in much the same way, tire marks at a scene can, too. Tires, like shoes, have treads on the bottom of them, with each brand having its own distinctive look. Just like you can differentiate a New Balance sneaker from a pair of Pumas, a Firestone tire will have a slightly different tread from a Goodyear—and the tire on a mountain bike will look very different from that of a regular 10-speed. Similarly, just as you'd expect the foot of a small woman weighing 100 pounds to leave a different impression from that of a 300-pound basketball player like Shaquille O'Neal, the tire marks from a Hummer are going to be noticeably different from those left by a Toyota.

There are two basic types of tire mark **impressions** that can be left at a crime scene: tire prints and skid marks. Tire prints are what a normally rolling tire leaves as a car drives down a street, after having rolled over something sticky or wet. Tire tracks will exhibit the tire tread pattern clearly and can be matched to a tire easily. Skid marks occur when a car has had the brakes applied suddenly. The wheel has stopped turning, the tires have locked, but the car has had such momentum, it keeps moving forward. So the tire leaves a rubber residue on the road.

Skid marks can provide investigators with some solid clues. By carefully examining skid marks and applying a mathematical formula, investigators can actually determine how fast the vehicle that made the skid marks was traveling. This can be particularly helpful at the scene of a hit-and-run vehicle accident, or when trying to track the movements of a getaway car.

Tires—like fingers and feet—can tell a skilled detective a great deal. It's just a matter of knowing how to listen!

What You Do

Part I. Slip-Sliding Away

1. First, ask your rookie friends to arrive at a specified location on their bikes. With your spray bottle filled with water, gently mist their bikes' wheels. You don't need to soak the tires, but you want to make sure they're damp enough so that they'll pick up an extra layer of dirt or dust.
2. Now tell your friends to ride around and patrol

the area for about a minute. Make sure they're on concrete or another hard surface. (And if they happen to splash through a muddy puddle or two, so much the better!) While they're patrolling, write down each rookie's name on separate sheets of white paper.

3. When they ride back toward you, flip the paper over so their names are face down, and have each rookie drive his bike over the piece of paper you've designated specifically for him.
4. Shuffle those papers—name side down—so you can't tell who put which tire print on which sheet of paper. Next, take out your magnifying glass and examine the tread marks left on each print.
5. Now examine the wheels on your friends' bikes. Can you match each tire to its mark? When you feel confident that you made the right match, flip the papers over to check the names to see if you were correct!

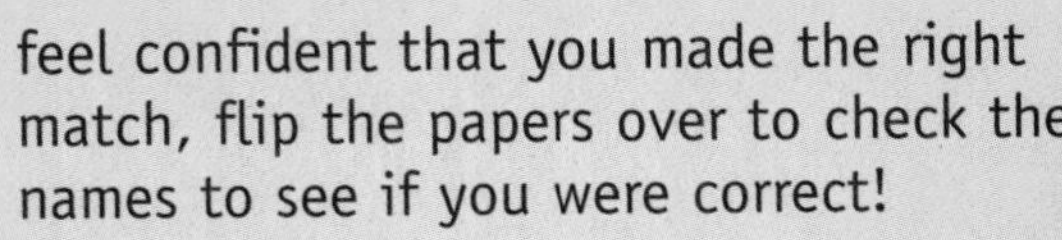

Part II. Cast-or-Oil?

Want a permanent record of your tire treads? Like you did with your footprints in *Case File #11: Shoes from Paris...Plaster of Paris!* you can make a mold of your treads by casting it in plaster.

1. First, ride your bike through a dirt-covered area, then set up your cardboard mold around the tire track, just like you did in *Case File #11: Shoes from Paris...Plaster of Paris!*
2. With your senior detective, get your plaster of Paris mixture together and pour it into the mold.
3. Wait an hour, then lift the cast from the ground and peel away the cardboard mold. Now take your paintbrush and brush away the remaining traces of mud. Your treads are preserved forever!

What's the Real Deal?

You should have seen in this activity, rookie, how a careful examination of tire tracks can help you to place a particular vehicle at a crime scene. Whether it's a car, truck, motorcycle, or bicycle—every vehicle out there has tires that come in contact with the ground. And so, if they drive through mud or some other sticky substance, they will leave a mark that can be matched to a suspect's particular mode of transportation. It's just a matter of some careful observation, and then some patient comparison. Because if you can place a suspect's vehicle at a crime scene, then there's a good chance he was there, too!

In real life, the detectives that most often rely on evidence of this type are those who investigate vehicle crimes. "Auto crime" and "highway safety" detectives spend their time examining the scene of vehicle accidents, hit-and-run incidents, and other crime scenes involving automobiles. These detectives are experts in tire track evidence of all sorts. What might look to a regular police officer like an innocent skid mark on the road will often tell a whole different story to a trained auto crime detective. It's just another example of the specialized knowledge that detectives bring to the job every day!

Case File #13

Tool Time!

Stuff You'll Need

- A pizza box or old shoebox
- Stapler
- Fellow rookie
- Screwdriver
- Scissors
- Fork
- Piece of wood
- Pen
- Sticky notes

You know, rookie, when a home is burglarized, one thing is certain: The thief had to get into that house somehow! Though this might seem like a "no brainer," it's a detail that detectives examine very closely because, at the point of entry, a perpetrator often leaves behind many clues. You already know about the likelihood of a **perp** leaving **fingerprints** at the scene—but if the burglarized house was locked, the perp had to have somehow got by that lock, too. And therefore, he left behind some additional helpful evidence!

When examining the way a lock was broken or a window was forced open, police look for **tool marks.** Tool marks occur when someone uses a hard object of some sort to force open a door or window—and, in so doing, leaves behind indentations or scuff marks. By carefully examining these marks, investigators can often determine exactly what type of tool was used in the crime. Then, if that particular tool can be found, there's a chance a suspect can be linked to it!

But before you can tie a suspect to a tool mark, the first step is to identify the tool itself. It takes practice—there are a lot of tools out there!

Ready to give it a try?

What You Do

Part I. Marking Your Territory

1. Take the empty pizza or shoebox and staple it shut by putting a couple of staples around the box's side. Then punch a few staples into the top of the box as well.

2. Now hand your rookie friend the following tools: a screwdriver, a pair of scissors, and a fork. While you wait in another room, tell her to remove the staples on the side of the box with one of the tools, and the staples on the top of the box with one of the other tools. (Be sure to tell her to be careful using the tools! You don't want her to hurt herself!) Remind her not to tell you which tools she plans on using!
3. When she's finished, come back into the room and start examining the tool marks she left while doing her work. Look at the distinguishing features of the tool marks. Can you match the marks on the *side* of the box to the tool she used to remove the staples? How about on the *top* of the box?

4. When you're done, grab a new box and switch roles. (If you don't have another box, you might just turn over the one you have.) As you remove the staples, do you notice how the tools you use leave their unique marks on the box?

Part II. Body of Evidence

1. First, assemble a group of tools from around your house. Try to gather tools you know will be tough enough to leave marks on a piece of wood (ask a senior detective for a spare piece of lumber or plywood). Be creative!
2. Then, after you leave the room, instruct your fellow rookie to start scraping, banging, cutting, or prying against the wood's surface with all the tools she has. (You don't need to have any staples in the wood—just let her mix up the tools, and bang away!) As always, be careful when you and your friends are using the tools, so you don't hurt yourselves. Also remind your friend to leave a little bit of space between marks, so that a clear picture of the tool marks is created.

3. When you return to the room, see if you can match up the tools to the marks they left on the wood. Under each mark that you identify on the surface of the wood, write down on a sticky note the tool you used to achieve it. You now have a permanent record of a whole catalogue of tool marks, which you can use as a reference in the future!

More From Detective Squad

Want to learn more about tool marks?

You can—when you head to **www.scholastic.com/detective**!

What's the Real Deal?

Did you see in this activity, rookie, how the various tools each left their own unique mark on the cardboard box or wood? Depending on the motion that was used to create them—and the tool involved—tool marks can be identified by looking at a "catalogue," or file of tool mark types. This is a great help in an investigation because detectives can reference their record of tool marks to see if the evidence at a crime scene matches a particular tool type. That's the purpose of the banged-up wood you examined. It's a catalogue of tool marks that you can use in the future.

Very often, detectives investigating a burglary will be able to tell—just by looking at tool marks—that the perp's method-of-entry is similar to that used in other burglaries in the area. That could mean detectives have a "pattern" on their hands—a series of similar crimes committed by what is probably the same perp. Now, all these crimes can be viewed together, and all the clues at all the crime scenes can be grouped into one big case. Because perps will often use the same methods over and over (especially if they worked!), tool marks can often be the key for detectives to use to link the crimes in a pattern together. Those random scratches and scrapes can be the biggest mistake a perp ever makes!

On the Job: At Work with Sergeant Priscilla Green

Las Vegas Metropolitan Police Department, Las Vegas, Nevada

Sergeant Priscilla Green of the Las Vegas, Nevada, Metropolitan Police Department is the supervisor in a special detective squad known as the "Tourist Safety" unit. Along with the ten detectives she surpervises, Sergeant Green spends her days prowling the Las Vegas casinos and the famous Las Vegas "Strip" (otherwise known as Las Vegas Boulevard).

Working in plain-clothes, Sergeant Green and her "Tourist Safety" squad are on the lookout for **perps** who prey on tourists. These perps commit "distraction crimes"—that is, they steal from the victim while the vic is being distracted. Some of these perps are very skilled pickpockets and con men, and it takes an expert detective to nail them!

Sergeant Green and her team generally start their day around 2:00 p.m. "We usually start with a briefing, talk to the day shift, see what they've been working on. We find out what's been happening on the Strip." A big part of the team's success comes from their ability to blend in. "We dress like tourists, work the crowds, and see what we can see. We're trying to catch them in the act."

Because pickpockets see crowds of distracted tourists as easy prey, Sergeant Green and her team know to focus on big events that draw a lot of people. "The pickpockets love big events, so we'll go where the pickpockets go."

But the work Sergeant Green and her squad do is not just about pickpockets. "We do anything that affects tourists. For instance, we recently had a burglary of over one million dollars in jewelry from a tourist's hotel room. We had the scene sealed off, the crime scene unit came and dusted for **prints**, and we did an investigation. We checked the hotel's video surveillance cameras. Eventually, we made an ID, and we currently have him in custody."

Like most detectives, Sergeant Green started out on patrol as a uniformed first responder. Now, as sergeant, she works keeping Las Vegas's major industry—tourism—safe. With her interesting specialized career, she's an excellent detective to get some expert advice from. So listen up, rookie!

"With this job, your life experiences really come into play. You have to know how to talk to people, and to use your common sense. Eventually, with time and practice, you learn how to *read* people—you can look at them, and just about tell what they're going to do! So you want to be as sharp as possible. Here, then, is my main advice: Get as much education as you can.

"Oh, and one last thing: Keep up with your writing skills. Detectives write a *lot* of reports!"

Case of the Half-Baked Burglary

Hey, rookie—there's been a burglary at the local bakery, and someone stole a lot of *dough*!

It seems that sometime during the night, two **perps** got into the Devine Bakery and broke open the cash register. But they made a little too much noise. They didn't realize that the owner, Mr. Devine himself, lives right upstairs. When he came down to see about all the commotion, the perps ran off!

Mr. Devine caught just a glimpse of two perps fleeing the scene—then he called the police. When the first responders arrived, they made sure no one was hurt, then secured the area. Now you catch the case, rookie, and arrive to find the below crime scene.

This is a picture of the interior of the Devine Bakery. Using your magnifying glass, examine the **print** and **impression** evidence very carefully!

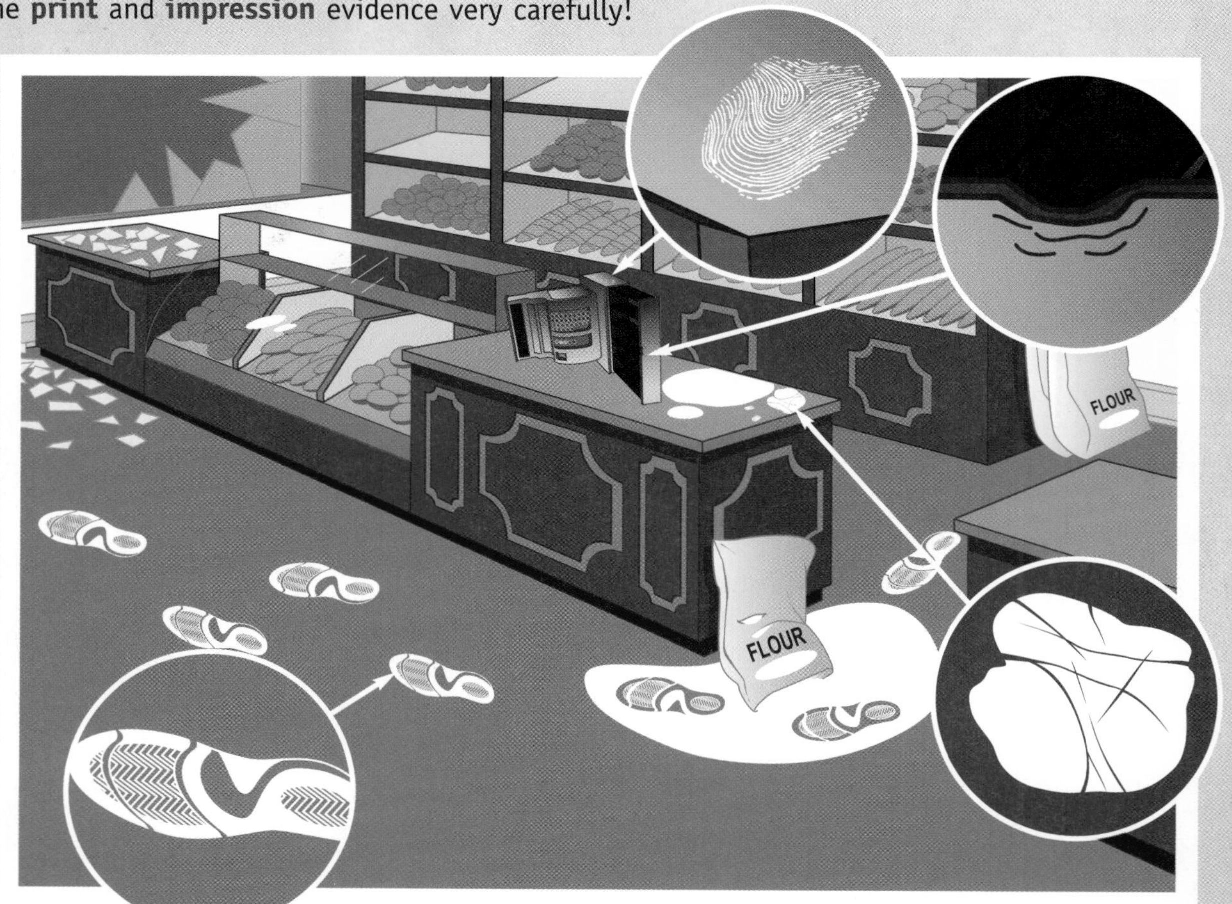

Okay, rookie—got a good idea of your evidence so far?

Here's more: Apparently, after the perps fled the scene on foot, they jumped into a car and sped off. Standing on the corner was Erin Henderson, who tells you the following during your witness interview: "Well, detective, I was standing near the corner when the car came screeching down the block, then turned just after it passed me. I saw two people in the car. They were both in the front seat. The driver was a white man in his early twenties, I think, and the passenger might have been an African-American man who was maybe a little younger."

You realize that the exterior of the bakery could have important evidence, so you expand your crime scene. Check out the rest of the scene below. See anything important?

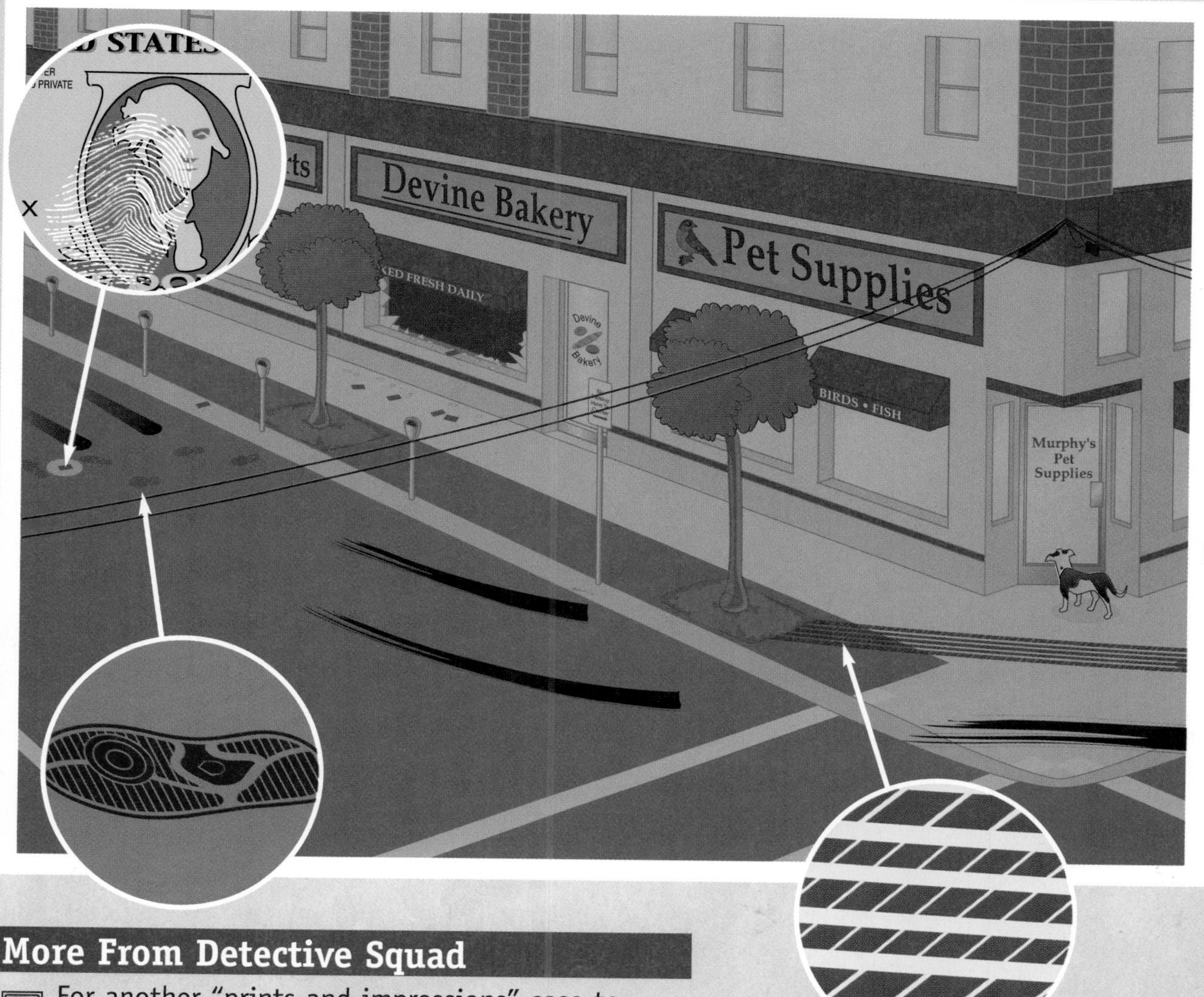

More From Detective Squad

For another "prints and impressions" case to solve, log on to **www.scholastic.com/detective**!

Rookie—time to use your fingerprint and impression skills to solve the case! Examine the pictures below. Can you match the clues with the evidence?

Fingerprints. Which of the following *two* index fingerprints were found at the scene?

Whorl

Loop

Plain Arch

Tented Arch

Tool Marks. Which tool was used in this crime?

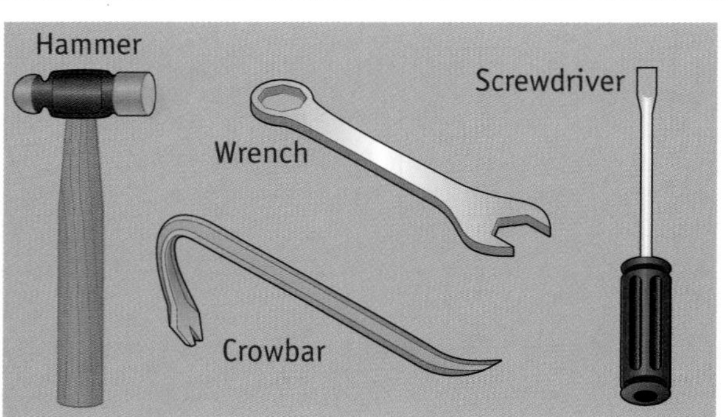

Palm Print. Can you match the palm print taken from the scene to any of the suspects (you'll see who they are on the next page)?

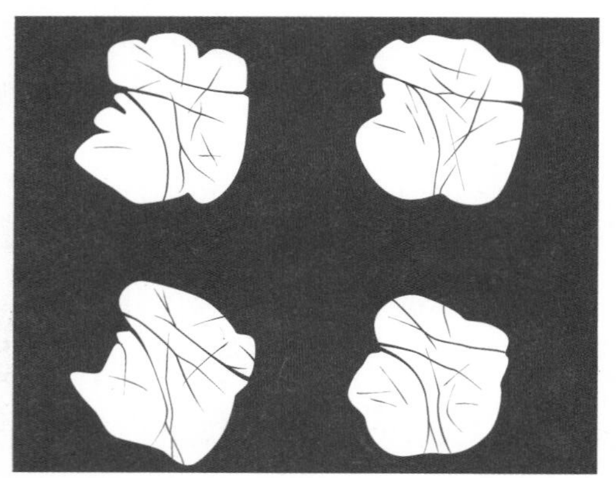

Tire Tracks. The tire tracks from which of these cars was found at the scene?

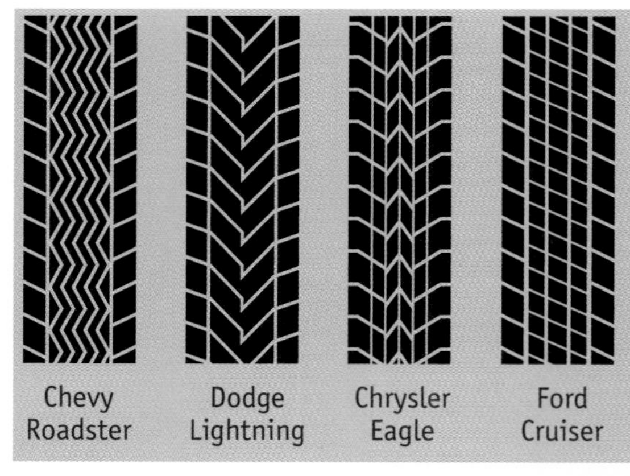

Footprints. Which *two* footprints were found at the scene?

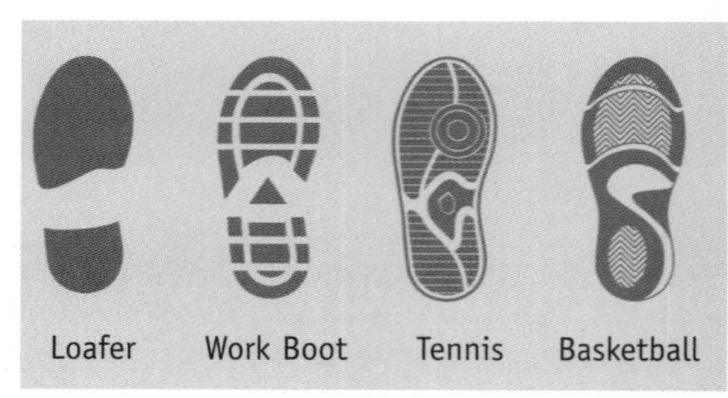

Think you matched the evidence? Well, not so fast, rookie! You still need to see who all this evidence points to!

Below are four suspects you've developed in the case. Some have tools "on" them when you pick them up, some don't. Some own cars, some don't. Using all your evidence, which *two* suspects are you going to *collar* (that is, *arrest*)?

Suspects.

1.	2.	3.	4.

John Tonelli	**Christopher Druckman**	**Pedro Morales**	**Ryan Lang**
Index-finger print: Plain Arch	Index-finger print: Loop	Index-finger print: Whorl	Index-finger print: Tented Arch
Tool possessed: Hammer	Tool possessed: Crowbar	Tool possessed: Screwdriver	Tool possessed: None
Shoes he's wearing: Loafers	Shoes he's wearing: Tennis Shoes	Shoes he's wearing: Work Boots	Shoes he's wearing: Basketball Sneakers
Car owned: None	Car owned: Ford Cruiser	Car owned: Chrysler Eagle	Car owned: Dodge Lightning

CASE CLOSED

(Answer Key)

Case File #1: Keep Your Ear to the Ground ***pages 9–11***

Part I. Why are fingerprints better for detectives to use than ear prints? Well, ask yourself, rookie: How many perps do you think leave ear prints at the scene of a crime? If they did—it would be an awfully strange crime!

Case File #4: Analyze This!
pages 19–21, Part I.

D

Part II. The perp's fingerprint can be classified as a whorl pattern.

C

Case File #7: Forge Ahead! ***pages 28–29***

Part III. Those prints were probably made by the bank employees who handled the check!

Case File #8: Go to Your Room! ***pages 30–31***

If you dusted places like the door, doorknob, window, and windowsill—excellent job, rookie, you covered the points of entry!

CASE CLOSED (continu

But there's more than just getting in. As you probably figured out, a perp in a home burglary is generally looking for any kind of valuables—only problem is, he doesn't know where they are! So he'll go through drawers, look under the bed, check the closet—anywhere something valuable might be. So...did you dust the drawer handles? The closet door? How about the edge of the bed? Maybe the perp tried to go on-line and access personal information about you (a good way to learn someone's bank account or credit card numbers). For that reason, the computer keyboard can be a good spot to dust (if you do that, however, be careful—you don't want to get powder in your keyboard!). If you've got any bags in your room—say, a school bag or a gym bag—the zippers are a good place to check. Any place a perp is likely to have put his hands is fair game!

And remember: Once in, the perp's got to get out! Did he leave the same way he got in? Not always! So just because there were prints at the window (his way in, say), he might have left by the door. Or even if he *did* go back out the window—by turning himself around and lowering himself out—he would have touched different areas, leaving additional prints. The key to all this is to examine the room very carefully—then try to figure out what the perp did while there. With a little imagination and good detecting, you're sure to find those prints!

Case File #9: See You Later, Gaitor *pages 32–33*

Part I. When you walk backward, you don't take as big steps as you do when you walk forward.

Part II. Impressions in sand can disappear pretty quickly!

Case File #10: Let Your Footprints Do the Talking! *page 34*

1. **C:** This person was walking, rookie—and then started running. See how the distance between the footprints increases about halfway through? And is deeper at the front, under the person's toes when they're running? This is because the person suddenly started taking longer strides and striking the ground harder with their toes.
2. **E:** Did you figure out what made that strange track off to the side of the footprints, rookie? Well, think like a detective: What does a person who only walks on one foot need? How about crutches?
3. **B:** The small feet walking are a child's feet. But off to the side? A very big dog!
4. **A:** The key here was to pick up that the single, continuous track was made by a wheel. If you got that—then figuring out that this was someone cruising along on a scooter was easy!
5. **D:** Well, there are a few things we can pick up from these tracks, rookie. First of all, we know he's probably a basketball player. Chances are this is a male. He must have just walked through a puddle, so his shoes are wet. That's why the prints fade as he walks.

Case of the Half-Baked Burglary *pages 44–47*

Well, rookie—if you arrested Christopher Druckman and Ryan Lang, you got your men! Let's see why:

Fingerprints: Did you see that the loop found on the cash register matched Druckman, and the tented arch found on the dollar bill matched Lang?

Tool Marks: Crowbar. Did you match the crowbar to the marks left on the cash register?

Footprints: The footprints found inside the store are a direct match for Ryan Lang's basketball sneakers. And the footprints outside the store match Christopher Druckman's tennis shoes—right down to the little "circle" imprint that indicates a pebble stuck in the tread!

Tire Tracks: Were you able to match the tire tracks found outside the store, after the vehicle turned, to the Ford Cruiser? And who do we know owns a Ford Cruiser? Chris Druckman!

Palm Print: Ah, a catch—*none* of the samples match to the palm print found at the scene! That means that this print must have been there already—probably, it matches to Mr. Devine himself! Were you fooled, rookie?

But wait a minute, rookie—the two perps don't match the description of who your witness, Erin Henderson, told you she saw. Well...so what? If you examine the scene carefully, you'll see a long skid mark right where Henderson says she was standing (on the corner). And what does that long skidmark indicate? That's right—that the perps were traveling *very fast* when they passed her by. Remember, too, that it was night, which would also have made it hard to get a good look at the perps.